Herodotus
and the Explorers of the Classical Age

General Editor

William H. Goetzmann
Jack S. Blanton, Sr., Chair in History
   University of Texas at Austin

Consulting Editor

Tom D. Crouch
Chairman, Department of Aeronautics
   National Air and Space Museum
   Smithsonian Institution

WORLD EXPLORERS

Herodotus
and the Explorers of the Classical Age

Ann Gaines

Introductory Essay by Michael Collins

CHELSEA HOUSE PUBLISHERS

New York · Philadelphia

On the cover Map of the ancient world by Posidonius

Chelsea House Publishers
Editorial Director Richard Rennert
Executive Managing Editor Karyn Gullen Browne
Executive Editor Sean Dolan
Copy Chief Robin James
Picture Editor Adrian G. Allen
Art Director Bob Mitchell
Manufacturing Director Gerald Levine
Systems Manager Lindsey Ottman
Production Coordinator Marie Claire Cebrián-Ume

World Explorers
Senior Editor Sean Dolan

Staff for HERODOTUS
Editorial Assistant Robert Green
Picture Researcher Pat Burns
Senior Designer Basia Niemczyc

First printing

1 3 5 7 9 8 6 4 2

Library of Congress Cataloging-in-Publication Data

Gaines, Ann.
Herodotus and the explorers of the Classical age / Ann Gaines.
p. cm.—(World explorers)
Includes bibliographical references and index.
Summary: Discusses the accounts of Greek historian Herodotus and the exploration of the world in which he lived.
ISBN 0-7910-1293-X
       0-7910-1323-5 (pbk.)
1. Mediterranean region—Discovery and exploration—Juvenile literature. 2. Herodotus. History. [1. Herodotus. 2. History, Ancient. 3. Mediterranean Region—Discovery and exploration.] I. Title. II. Series.   92-47086
DE31.G35 1993   CIP
909'.09822—dc20   AC

CONTENTS

WORLD EXPLORERS

THE EARLY EXPLORERS

Herodotus and the Explorers of the Classical Age
Marco Polo and the Medieval Explorers
The Viking Explorers

THE FIRST GREAT AGE OF DISCOVERY

Jacques Cartier, Samuel de Champlain, and the Explorers of Canada
Christopher Columbus and the First Voyages to the New World
From Coronado to Escalante: The Explorers of the Spanish Southwest
Hernando de Soto and the Explorers of the American South
Sir Francis Drake and the Struggle for an Ocean Empire
Vasco da Gama and the Portuguese Explorers
La Salle and the Explorers of the Mississippi
Ferdinand Magellan and the Discovery of the World Ocean
Pizarro, Orellana, and the Exploration of the Amazon
The Search for the Northwest Passage

THE SECOND GREAT AGE OF DISCOVERY

Roald Amundsen and the Quest for the South Pole
Daniel Boone and the Opening of the Ohio Country
Captain James Cook and the Explorers of the Pacific
The Explorers of Alaska
John Charles Frémont and the Great Western Reconnaissance
Alexander von Humboldt, Colossus of Exploration
Lewis and Clark and the Route to the Pacific
Alexander Mackenzie and the Explorers of Canada
Robert Peary and the Quest for the North Pole
Zebulon Pike and the Explorers of the American Southwest
John Wesley Powell and the Great Surveys of the American West
Jedediah Smith and the Mountain Men of the American West
Henry Stanley and the European Explorers of Africa
Lt. Charles Wilkes and the Great U.S. Exploring Expedition

THE THIRD GREAT AGE OF DISCOVERY

Apollo to the Moon
The Explorers of the Undersea World
The First Men in Space
The Mission to Mars and Beyond
Probing Deep Space

CHELSEA HOUSE PUBLISHERS

Into the Unknown

Michael Collins

It is difficult to define most eras in history with any precision, but not so the space age. On October 4, 1957, it burst on us with little warning when the Soviet Union launched *Sputnik*, a 184-pound cannonball that circled the globe once every 96 minutes. Less than 4 years later, the Soviets followed this first primitive satellite with the flight of Yury Gagarin, a 27-year-old fighter pilot who became the first human to orbit the earth. The Soviet Union's success prompted President John F. Kennedy to decide that the United States should "land a man on the moon and return him safely to earth" before the end of the 1960s. We now had not only a space age but a space race.

I was born in 1930, exactly the right time to allow me to participate in Project Apollo, as the U.S. lunar program came to be known. As a young man growing up, I often found myself too young to do the things I wanted—or suddenly too old, as if someone had turned a switch at midnight. But for Apollo, 1930 was the perfect year to be born, and I was very lucky. In 1966 I enjoyed circling the earth for three days, and in 1969 I flew to the moon and laughed at the sight of the tiny earth, which I could cover with my thumbnail.

How the early explorers would have loved the view from space! With one glance Christopher Columbus could have plotted his course and reassured his crew that the world was indeed round. In 90 minutes Magellan could have looked down at every port of call in the *Victoria*'s three-year circumnavigation of the globe. Given a chance to map their route from orbit, Lewis and Clark could have told President Jefferson that there was no easy Northwest Passage but that a continent of exquisite diversity awaited their scrutiny.

In a physical sense, we have already gone to most places that we can. That is not to say that there are not new adventures awaiting us in the sea or on the red plains of Mars, but more important than reaching new places will be understanding those we have already visited. There are vital gaps in our understanding of how our planet works as an ecosystem and how our planet fits into the infinite order of the universe. The next great age may well be the age of assimilation, in which we use microscope and telescope to evaluate what we have discovered and put that knowledge to use. The adventure of being first to reach may be replaced by the satisfaction of being first to grasp. Surely that is a form of exploration as vital to our well-being, and perhaps even survival, as the distinction of being the first to explore a specific geographical area.

The explorers whose stories are told in the books of this series did not just sail perilous seas, scale rugged mountains, traverse blistering deserts, dive to the depths of the ocean, or land on the moon. Their voyages and expeditions were journeys of mind as much as of time and distance, through which they—and all of mankind—were able to reach a greater understanding of our universe. That challenge remains, for all of us. The imperative is to see, to understand, to develop knowledge that others can use, to help nurture this planet that sustains us all. Perhaps being born in 1975 will be as lucky for a new generation of explorer as being born in 1930 was for Neil Armstrong, Buzz Aldrin, and Mike Collins.

The Reader's Journey

William H. Goetzmann

This volume is one of a series that takes us with the great explorers of the ages on bold journeys over the oceans and the continents and into outer space. As we travel along with these imaginative and creative journeyers, we share their adventures and their knowledge. We also get a glimpse of that mysterious and inextinguishable fire that burned in the breast of men such as Magellan and Columbus—the fire that has propelled all those throughout the ages who have been driven to leave behind family and friends for a voyage into the unknown.

No one has satisfactorily explained the urge to explore, the drive to go to the "back of beyond." It is certain that it has been present in man almost since he began walking erect and first ventured across the African savannas. Sparks from that same fire fueled the transoceanic explorers of the Ice Age, who led their people across the vast plain that formed a land bridge between Asia and North America, and the astronauts and scientists who determined that man must reach the moon.

Besides an element of adventure, all exploration involves an element of mystery. We must not confuse exploration with discovery. Exploration is a purposeful human activity—a search for something. Discovery may be the end result of that search; it may also be an accident, as when Columbus found a whole new world while searching for the Indies. Often, the explorer may not even realize the full significance of what he has discovered, as was the case with Columbus. Exploration, on the other hand, is the product of a cultural or individual curiosity; it is a unique process that has enabled mankind to know and understand the world's oceans, continents, and polar regions. It is at the heart of scientific thinking. One of its most significant aspects is that it teaches people to ask the right questions; by doing so, it forces us to reevaluate what we think we know and understand. Thus knowledge progresses, and we are driven constantly to a new awareness and appreciation of the universe in all its infinite variety.

The motivation for exploration is not always pure. In his fascination with the new, man often forgets that others have been there before him. For example, the popular notion of the discovery of America overlooks the complex Indian civilizations that had existed there for thousands of years before the arrival of Europeans. Man's desire for conquest, riches, and fame is often linked inextricably with his quest for the unknown, but a story that touches so closely on the human essence must of necessity treat war as well as peace, avarice with generosity, both pride and humility, frailty and greatness. The story of exploration is above all a story of humanity and of man's understanding of his place in the universe.

The WORLD EXPLORERS series has been divided into four sections. The first treats the explorers of the ancient world, the Viking explorers of the 9th through the 11th centuries, and Marco Polo and the medieval explorers. The rest of the series is divided into three great ages of exploration. The first is the era of Columbus and Magellan: the period spanning the 15th and 16th centuries, which saw the discovery and exploration of the New World and the world ocean. The second might be called the age of science and imperialism, the era made possible by the scientific advances of the 17th century, which witnessed the discovery of the world's last two undiscovered continents, Australia and Antarctica, the mapping of all the continents and oceans, and the establishment of colonies all over the world. The third great age refers to the most ambitious quests of the 20th century—the probing of space and of the ocean's depths.

As we reach out into the darkness of outer space and other galaxies, we come to better understand how our ancestors confronted *oecumene*, or the vast earthly unknown. We learn once again the meaning of an unknown 18th-century sea captain's advice to navigators:

> And if by chance you make a landfall on the shores of another sea in a far country inhabited by savages and barbarians, remember you this: the greatest danger and the surest hope lies not with fires and arrows but in the quicksilver hearts of men.

At its core, exploration is a series of moral dramas. But it is these dramas, involving new lands, new people, and exotic ecosystems of staggering beauty, that make the explorers' stories not only moral tales but also some of the greatest adventure stories ever recorded. They represent the process of learning in its most expansive and vivid forms. We see that real life, past and present, transcends even the adventures of the starship *Enterprise*.

Conquest and Chronicles

On a stormy day late in the summer of 327 B.C., on the banks of the Hyphasis River, deep in the Runjau region of modern-day India, the conqueror and explorer we now refer to as Alexander the Great called his massive army to a halt after the latest hard day's march of a difficult campaign. To that point, Alexander, by birthright king of Macedon (an ancient kingdom on the Balkan Peninsula) and by force of arms captain-general of Greece, had led his 35,000 soldiers some 10,000 miles from their homes. It had been seven years since his troops had marched out of Pella, the Macedonian capital, east to the Dardanelles, the strait that connects the Aegean Sea with the Sea of Marmara and is often regarded as the dividing line between Europe and Asia. Bound to conquer the giant empire of Persia, Greece's foe for generations, Alexander's forces had sailed across the straits onto Persian soil, then fought their way south through territories encompassing the present-day nations of Turkey, Syria, Lebanon, and Israel, into Africa and the lands of Egypt and Libya, and then had battled their way back north and east across today's Jordan, Iraq, Iran, Afghanistan, and Pakistan and on into India. By the time they had reached the banks of the Hyphasis (known today as the Beas), Alexander had long since won the throne of Persia's Great King (and that of Egypt's pharaoh), but still he pushed his men on relentlessly, for he was driven by nothing less than the desire to rule the entire known world.

Alexander the Great, king of Macedon, explored and conquered the known world. "Alexander considered that he had come from the gods to be a general governor and reconciler of men," wrote the Greek biographer Plutarch.

Alexander's exploits won him such renown that legends about him can be found in virtually every language of Europe, the Middle East, and Central Asia. In many of the medieval romances written about him, Alexander meets, like many a great hero before him, all manner of mythological beasts and creatures said to inhabit the far places of the world. On the page from the medieval German illuminated manuscript seen here, Alexander encounters dog-headed men and bird-headed women.

By the time he reached the Hyphasis, Alexander was still a very young man, barely 28 years of age. Blond and clean-shaven, he was small by the standards of today but strong, with rippling muscles. A seasoned soldier, he was also one of the most learned men of his day—as a youth his tutors had included the philosopher Aristotle, one of history's most famous thinkers—but there seemed never to be enough battles and books to fulfill him. A born conqueror, he yearned always for more power and new lands to fall before him; a born explorer, he yearned always to know what lay beyond the next horizon. Now he seemed mesmerized by the Himalayas, the towering, snowcapped mountains visible in the far distance beyond the Hyphasis. Between the river and the peaks, he had heard, ran another, greater river, the Ganges, four miles wide, and beyond lay a beautiful, bountiful land, ruled by a rajah named Ksandrames, whose army of 400,000 men was backed by a pack of 4,000 fierce elephants. Alexander was determined to vanquish this Ksandrames in battle, and then, he dreamed, he and his men would conquer the Himalayas themselves and reach the Sea of the East, which was said to lie beyond. This would bring him, he believed, to the very eastern edge of the earth itself, for according to the best geographers of the day, including Aristotle, the world consisted of a single continent bound by high mountains and surrounded by a great wild ocean.

Alexander's men hardly shared their leader's fascination with the great beyond. They had marched now for 10 consecutive weeks in constant, torrential rain that did little to cool them and in fact seemed only to add to the stifling heat. Their clothes were falling to tatters on their bodies, and their armor was rusting. Many were now shaking and chilled from fever, and many more lived in terror of the strange, deadly animals—huge snakes, such as pythons and cobras, and ferocious, colorful cats, such as tigers—they had begun to encounter. Almost all had long since had their fill of exotic lands and longed to go home.

Mindful of the low morale of his men, Alexander tried to buoy their spirits by giving them leave to plunder the rich lands that bordered the Hyphasis. They returned with fortunes in jewels and gems but remained unappeased, for what good was treasure so far from home? Eager to press on, the next day Alexander summoned his officers, or Companions, as he called them, to discuss his strategy for completing his conquest of the world. "If any of you wish to know what limit may be set to this particular campaign," he said, "let me tell you that the area of country ahead of us, from here to the Ganges, is comparatively small. You will undoubtedly find that this ocean is connected with the Hyrcanian Sea [the ancients' name for the Caspian Sea], for the Great Stream of Ocean circles the earth. Moreover, I shall prove to you, my friends, that the Indian and Persian gulfs and the Hyrcanian Sea are all three connected and continuous. Our ships will sail round from the Persian Gulf to Libya as far as the Pillars of Hercules [the Strait of Gibraltar], whence all Libya to the eastward will soon be

Alexander leads his forces over the rugged Hindu Kush mountain range into India, where finally the reluctance of his men forced him to stop. "It is a lovely thing to live with courage and die leaving an everlasting fame," Alexander supposedly told his men in urging them onward.

ours, and all Asia too, and to this empire there will be no boundaries but what God himself has made for the entire world."

A shocked silence followed, broken at last by the words of Coenus, one of Alexander's most trusted Companions. "If there is one thing above all others that a successful man should know, it is when to stop," said the brave Coenus, and his words were followed by much spontaneous cheering. Enraged, Alexander stalked off to his tent, where

he stayed without emerging for three days. At the end of that time, he called for his prophets, seers, and soothsayers and ordered them to petition the gods for an omen. No less tired than the Great King's soldiers, they returned from their ceremonies to report that the gods did not wish Alexander and his army to cross the Hyphasis. To this, Alexander regretfully submitted, and he sat on the banks of the river he was destined never to cross and wept. Before turning back, he had 12 enormous sacrificial altars erected on the site so that future generations would regard this spot as his intended destination and not suspect that he had been disappointed in his desire to continue onward. Following a long and complicated series of religious rituals, Alexander and his army set off to the southwest and the Persian Gulf.

Scholars and students have long regarded Alexander the Great as one of history's most fascinating individuals. Military historians consider his great eastern expedition, filled as it was with victory after hard-fought victory, long sieges, tumultuous hand-to-hand battles, and quick cavalry strikes, one of the greatest military campaigns of all time. They regard his reign as one of the most enlightened in ancient history, pointing out that, unlike most conquerors, he allowed the peoples he subjugated to retain their own culture and aspired to bring peace to his empire. But Alexander the Great was more than a splendid general and enlightened despot: he is also recognized as one of history's most intrepid explorers, for his journey through western Asia took him ever deeper into lands previously unknown to the Greeks and Macedonians.

Today, as is true of so many of the explorers of the classical world and their journeys, there is much that remains unknown about even such an important and famous figure as Alexander. Through the discovery of artifacts from Alexander's age, archaeologists have provided many of the known details about his kingdom. Sadly, contemporary chronicles and records from Alexander's

time seem to be virtually nonexistent. Certainly, many of his contemporaries must have written about Alexander the Great, but these works have been lost. Instead, the primary sources for many of the details of his life are histories written by the Romans 400 years later and based on the lost Greek sources. Thus, many questions about his travels remain unanswered.

And so it is, unfortunately, with much of the exploration that took place during the classical age—the era when first the ancient Greeks and then the Romans dominated the

A Welsh illuminated manuscript from the Middle Ages shows Alexander fending off skin-clad, club-wielding giants. By the time he reached India, the real dangers of the campaign were much more frightening to his men than any imaginary terrors.

western world. Only a very few records remain of early exploring expeditions. This does not mean, however, that only a few exploring expeditions were undertaken by ancient peoples, but that we know of only a fraction of those voyages and journeys that did occur.

Why is this? In many cases, no records were made of important expeditions. Many of the explorers of the ancient world were probably illiterate, and others may have deliberately avoided making a record of their discoveries. For example, the Phoenicians, a seafaring people who dominated the Mediterranean several centuries before Alexander's time—the center of their empire was on the coast of present-day Lebanon—jealously guarded their geographic knowledge from all potential rivals. In other cases, records were made but have simply been lost.

To make the study of ancient exploration even more difficult, problems abound with the accounts of ancient voyages that do remain. In some cases, scholars simply cannot translate ancient documents to their complete satisfaction. In other instances, supposedly factual accounts of voyages include fantastic details, leaving us uncertain as to which parts of a story to believe. In still other cases, accounts generally accepted as true refer to locales that have proven difficult to identify, for any number of reasons: place names have changed, landmarks have disappeared or been destroyed, rivers have altered their course.

For all of these reasons, the chroniclers of the ancient voyages of exploration are in many ways as of great importance and interest as the explorers themselves, for without the words of the chroniclers, it would be as if the voyages never took place—or as if the voyagers had sailed or marched out of sight and never reappeared. Chroniclers have been important in each of the four great ages of exploration. If Antonio Pigafetta, the Venetian gentleman-adventurer who accompanied Ferdinand Magellan on his famous voyage of circumnavigation and wrote the only first-person account of the expedition, had perished with his captain in the Philippines, little would be known of Magellan's great adventure, for example. Marco Polo was derided as a fantasist by his fellow Venetians for his tales of his trip to the fabulous court of Kublai Khan; were it not for the account of his adventures penned for him by one Rusticello of Pisa, which enabled later generations to verify the essential accuracy of his story, Polo would be no more than a curious historical footnote. Latter-day explorers have been so keenly aware of the power of chroniclers to assure their fame that most of the great explorers of the 18th, 19th, and 20th centuries took pains to pen their own accounts of their exploits.

As regards the exploration of the ancient world, no chronicler is more important than Herodotus, the 5th-century B.C. Greek historian known as the Father of History. An explorer in his own right who as a young man traveled in Egypt (he went up the Nile as far as present-day Aswan), elsewhere in northern Africa, the Middle East, and even parts of Russia, Herodotus is best known for *Histories*, his multivolumed account of the wars between Greece and the Persian Empire for control of the ancient world of the West. Because the influence of Persia and Greece was so far-flung, extending over most of the "known" world of the time; and because Herodotus undertook the ambitious aim of providing the complete history of the two warring empires prior to their time of conflict, his book, which is regarded as the first great prose work of Western literature, serves as a kind of compendium of geographic, historical, and cultural information about the ancient world—the kind of information that explorers and travelers brought back with them from their journeys. Herodotus speculated on geographic puzzles that continued to intrigue explorers up to the modern era—the mystery of the source of the Nile, for example, of which he said "no one can give any account" for the river originates in the "wild beast region"—penned descriptive accounts

*Father of History, Father of Lies,
the 5th-century B.C. Greek historian Herodotus is both one of the
most respected and one of the most
reviled chroniclers of the ancient
world, lauded for his powers of
narrative and condemned for his
lack of accuracy. "I will proceed
with my history," wrote Herodotus, "telling the story as I go along
of small cities no less than of great.
For most of those which were great
once, are small today; and those
which used to be small were great
in my own time."*

of the flora, fauna, and human inhabitants of remote and
exotic lands, and recounted episodes of various exploratory
expeditions, such as the Phoenicians' circumnavigation of
Africa from the Indian Ocean to the Atlantic Ocean. On
every page of his work, he displayed the relentless curiosity
about other places and peoples that is the common

hallmark of explorers, no matter what age they live in. He possessed, as the scholar Aubrey de Selincourt has pointed out, the characteristic most required of explorers, whether their excursions take them to new lands or merely new realms of the intellect—"a delighted interest in the unpredictable variety of human existence."

Often criticized for the unreliability of some of his accounts, Herodotus is also much emulated; his style, method, and content have influenced countless historians, and for better or worse his books influenced European beliefs about the rest of the world for centuries. As his *Histories* constitute the most complete picture of the ancient world as it was known to its inhabitants, Herodotus may rightly be considered among its foremost explorers, and some of the spirit of his narrative informs all those who tell tales of the explorers of the classical age.

Exploring the Middle of the World

Between the converging continents of Africa, Asia, and Europe—the known world of the ancients—the Mediterranean Sea forms a vast water barrier, a virtual giant lake whose only contact with the rest of the world's oceans is its tiny outlet with the Atlantic Ocean at the Strait of Gibraltar, at the western edges of Africa and Europe. From Spain in the west to its easternmost reaches, the northern coastline of the Mediterranean is blessed with many natural protected harbors. Though there are fewer natural harbors and less favorable winds along the Mediterranean's African coasts or along the eastern region known as the Levant (generally the modern-day nations of Lebanon, Syria, and Israel), in general the Mediterranean Sea has long been a friendly place for the sailors who lived along its shores. There are only a few treacherous currents, and, in summer months, a constant favorable wind for sailing; it is possible to sail around the entire Mediterranean without ever leaving the sight of land or lacking for a safe harbor each night. In the classical age, the clean, unpolluted sea was home to an abundant variety of underwater life, yielding not only fish and other seafood but also treasures for barter: pearls and sponges and corals. In prehistoric times, the peoples who inhabited the areas around the Mediterranean rapidly became, from necessity,

This medieval mosaic depicts scenes from the Nile Delta in Egypt. The ancient Egyptians were among the first people to navigate the Mediterranean for the purpose of commerce.

adept sailors: the sea became the quickest and easiest way to travel and transport goods from one part of the Mediterranean world to another, and it almost immediately became the focus of Western civilization. Even its name bespeaks its importance in the worldview of ancient Europeans—Mediterranean means "middle of the land" and, by

This medieval Arabic map of the world illustrates the importance the Mediterranean and the Nile retained for the peoples of Europe and the Middle East.

extension, middle of the earth, and to ancient Europeans, the sea was such.

In the southeastern corner of the Mediterranean Sea lies the Nile Delta, a vast, abundant marsh where the Nile River empties after traveling thousands of miles northward from the mountains in the heartland of Africa. Here,

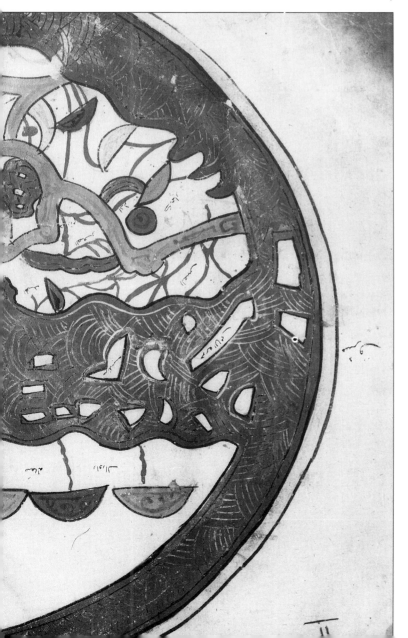

Egyptian forces (right) repel an invasion by southern tribesmen; a detail from a wall painting found in the tomb of Tutankhamen, who ruled in the 14th century B.C. Much of what we know about ancient Egyptian civilization and culture is derived from these murals.

beginning in about 3200 B.C., arose the great civilization of the ancient Egyptians, builders not only of the magnificent pyramids, mysterious wonders of the ancient world, but also of some of the first ships capable of transporting large cargoes of raw materials and finished goods from foreign markets around the Mediterranean Sea and as far away as Arabia and even India. The ships that the Egyptians used were made from the papyrus reeds that grew so abundantly in the Nile Delta. The oldest known illustrations of ships appear preserved in the tombs of the earliest pharaohs (the kings of ancient Europe); they show sickle-shaped reed boats that were constructed from bundles of papyrus stems lashed together, with each end of the boat

curving gracefully upward to a carved papyrus flower at the
stem and the stern. The ancestors and gods of the Egyptians
are always depicted riding in these reed boats, and the
whole history of the development of sailing ships in Egypt
and Phoenicia can be traced in these murals. An early
Greek tradition credits the invention of the large 50-oared
cargo ships that began plying the Mediterranean several
centuries before Herodotus to an Egyptian named Danaus.
With 25 oarsmen on each side, this sort of ship was large
enough for both ocean and river traffic and was capable of
carrying large loads.

The earliest recorded Egyptian sea voyage took place
during the reign of the Pharaoh Snefru around 3200 B.C. A

A kingfisher dives for prey in a papyrus swamp. The Egyptians used various parts of the papyrus plant as fuel, food, building material, fabric, twine, and paper.

mural from this period commemorates the return to Egypt from the Phoenician port of Byblos of 40 ships, each loaded with 100 cubits of cedar wood. By this time, Egypt had established regular maritime commerce with Phoenicia, to obtain lumber, and with Crete, to obtain tin.

Over the next several thousand years, as the murals show, Egypt developed and refined the hollow wooden boat, which soon became the vessel of choice for its sailors. At first, Egyptian boat builders who worked with wood, which was more durable but less flexible than papyrus, slavishly imitated the shape of the reed boats, even to the extent of carving the high and sweeping curves of the bow and stern. These wooden boats were lashed together with ropes sewn through holes drilled into the wooden planks. Archaelogists have discovered, in the tomb of the pharaoh Cheops, a well-preserved 147-foot wooden boat from this period. The ropes holding the vessel together had rotted and dissolved, but when the planks were carefully rejoined with new ropes, the ship that was first constructed some 2,700 years before the birth of Christ sprang to life, revealing a graceful and streamlined shape that closely resembled the Viking ships of 3,000 years later. Interestingly, the boat lacked any internal supports or braces for the outside hull. The waters of the Nile were presumably calm enough to make such structural supports unnecessary, but the Mediterranean must have presented a much more formidable challenge. Though reed boats continued to be used, by 1500 B.C. most of the vessels portrayed in the murals were made of wood. Only hunting barges or the small fishing boats used by poorer people continued to be constructed of papyrus.

The Egyptians established trade routes not only in the Mediterranean but also along the east coast of Africa and across the Red Sea on the Arabian Peninsula. Before about 1400 B.C., during the reign of Queen Hatshepsut, the Red Sea was known chiefly through hearsay and legend as the watery expanse separating Egypt from the mythical kingdom of Punt, land of rare and precious spices. (Punt was in all likelihood either the northern coast of present-day Somalia or, across the Gulf of Aden from Somalia, the coast of present-day Yemen on the Arabian Peninsula.)

Some hieroglyphics from the time of ancient Egypt's Middle Kingdom (approximately 2000–1500 B.C.) tell of a fantastic voyage beyond the kingdom of Punt made by a courageous Egyptian merchant who sailed down the Arabian coast until his ship was blown off course by a sudden storm and wrecked. The merchant, the sole survivor of this misfortune, was washed up on the shore of a bountiful island that contained the spices and rare woods of the fabled Orient. Life was easy there until the castaway was attacked by a huge serpent that spoke to him in human speech. When the sailor told the sorrowful story of his shipwreck to the snake, the reptile consoled the man and predicted to him that soon a ship would come to rescue him. When the ship did arrive, the talking snake revealed that he was actually an incarnation of the prince of Punt, gave the castaway merchant a full load of spices and incenses, and promised him that he would receive a steady returning wind and would arrive in Egypt in two months. The happy ending of the story tells of the merchant returning successfully home and giving all of the gifts he had received to the government.

For all its fantastic elements, the story may be rooted in fact—the discovery by the Egyptians of the monsoon winds, which make trade and travel throughout the Indian Ocean possible. Each group of ancient explorers— the Egyptians, the Minoans, the Phoenicians, and the Greeks—had to rediscover the secret of these winds.

Sometime around 1322 B.C., Queen Hatshepsut sent a great naval expedition to Somalia; to Socotra, even farther along the coast of East Africa; to the stark, mountainous coast of southern Arabia known as the Hadramut; and possibly even beyond that, to the Kuria Muria Islands, off present-day Oman. The great success of this expedition was recorded in the mural reliefs of the temple at Deir el-Bahri in Egypt, which show not the usual humped cattle from Somalia but the smooth-backed cattle of southern Arabia in the returning vessels, as well as whole incense trees that

(continued on page 41)

A Number of Remarkable Things

Egyptian prisoners of war, fettered at the elbows.

About Egypt I shall have a great deal more to relate because of the number of remarkable things which the country contains, and because of the fact that more monuments which beggar description are to be found there than anywhere else in the world," wrote Herodotus in Book Two of his *Histories*. The great Greek historian, himself one of the first European explorers of Egypt, was writing in the 5th century B.C., but modern scholars, archaeologists, and historians have found little reason to quibble with the Father of Lies' characterization of Egypt as a land of marvelous antiquities. Among the wonders uncovered there by modern researchers are the wall paintings found in many ancient tombs. Commissioned by wealthy Egyptians, these murals were intended to portray, in as much detail as possible, the everyday material life of the deceased, who expected to enjoy a much similar existence in the afterlife. "The scenes therefore show him engaged in all the pursuits of his daily life," explains the art historian Charles K. Wilkinson, "such as surveying his estate or overseeing the branding of his cattle, and enjoying with his family all the good things of this world. . . . Since the wall paintings depict in detail each tomb owner in his own earthly environment and occupations, the range of subjects is indeed comprehensive, covering almost every phase of ancient Egyptian life and the parts played by its people, from the highest official to the humblest servant."

Many Egyptian deities were portrayed with the heads of animals. Herodotus gave the Egyptians credit for originating many aspects of Greek religion. "But it was only—if I may so put it— the day before yesterday that the Greeks came to know the origin and form of the various gods," he wrote.

Egyptian gods and goddesses were often portrayed in incarnations as animals, especially as cats, hares, and serpents.

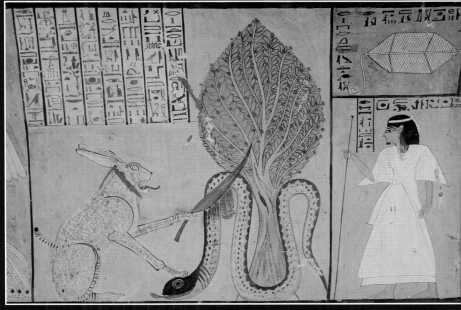

Egyptian women leave offerings of food and drink for Osiris, the god of life. Osiris is often portrayed with green skin, indicating his role as a god of vegetation.

A waterfowl in a papyrus swamp. According to Herodotus, [animals] as there are [in Egypt]—both wild and tame—are exception held to be sacred." Birds were held in especially hig by Herodotus's account, it was a crime punishable by death hawk or an ibis.

(continued from page 32)

resemble the kind grown at Dhofar on the Arabian coast. Queen Hatshepsut's daring expedition made reality from the story of the shipwrecked merchant and the prince of Punt; the murals show that a bountiful trade with the land of Punt became real and greatly profited the kingdom of Egypt. From this time on, a yearly Egyptian trade took place with the entire Arabian Peninsula.

The next great sailors to emerge from the region of the eastern Mediterranean came from the many islands sur-

Ravaged by time, the Great Sphinx still stands guard outside its master's tomb at Giza. In various forms and incarnations, sphinxes were a common image in many of the cultures of the ancient world.

rounding Greece and the Aegean Sea near the coast of Asia
Minor. The peoples of these islands had migrated there
from the mainland of Asia as early as 6000 B.C. For
thousands of years these peoples, protected by the isolation
the seas provided, developed their civilization in peace.
Based on the cultivation of their fertile lands and the
maritime trade of their capable fishermen and merchants,
this civilization had its center on the island of Crete and
its capital palace at Knossos.

Thousands of years later, the Greeks fashioned many
myths about the splendor and wealth of this island civilization and its magnificent palace at Knossos. According to
the Greek legends, the greatest king of these peoples was
King Minos, and so these peoples became known to the
Greeks as the Minoans.

The Minoans inhabited many of the islands around
Crete and built palaces and cities on most of them, but
certainly the most magnificent of their structures was the
Palace of Knossos. Constructed around 1900 B.C. atop the
rubble of many older Minoan dwellings that had been built
on the same site thousands of years ago, the palace had no
fortifications or outside walls for protection. Living on an
island certainly provided the Minoans with a natural
barrier to foreign invaders, but the absence of walls or
palisades indicates as well that the Minoans enjoyed an
especially secure society. Like many structures in the
Mediterranean, the palace of Knossos was built around a
central rectangular courtyard, in this case 2,000 square feet
in area. The palace itself measured 500 feet by 350 feet and
contained magnificent murals and frescoes depicting
various scenes of Minoan life. Intricately fashioned gold
rings and valuable jewelry have been discovered in the
ruins of the palace, including works of lapis lazuli, the
beautiful blue stone that came only from Afghanistan.
Because the islands of the Minoan civilization could never
have supplied all of the resources needed to construct and
decorate the palace, there is no doubt that the Minoans

had established an extensive network of trading partners throughout the Mediterranean, and they derived much of their wealth from this commerce. The boats of these Minoan sailors were wooden vessels with keels and ribs—the same kind of internal braces used in modern ship design. These supports were used to strengthen the Minoan ships so that they could more easily withstand the rigors of open-sea voyages.

The Minoan and Egyptian civilizations had extensive contact with one another as early as 3000 B.C. The Minoans used two routes to reach Egypt by sea: due south from their ports until they reached the African coast, then eastward to the Nile Delta; or eastward to Phoenicia and then south and west along the coast. Minoan ships were employed by the Egyptian pharaoh Tothmes III to aid him in his invasion of Syria around 1500 B.C.; Egyptian frescoes from about this time also show ships arriving in Egypt from foreign ports laden with the trade goods of the world. These ships and men are of a distinctly Cretan type, and the trade goods also appear to be of the same style of manufacture as artifacts of the ancient Minoan civilization found on the islands around Crete.

The Minoans did not confine their explorations in the service of commerce to the eastern Mediterranean; there is strong evidence of the early presence of the Minoans in the western Mediterranean and even beyond the Strait of Gibraltar into the Atlantic Ocean. In the ancient world, the only source of a pumicelike stone known as liparite was two active volcanoes, Stromboli and Vulcans, located in the Aeolians, a group of seven small islands, to the northwest of Sicily. As liparite is part of the beautiful stonework of the Palace of Knossos, it is obvious that the Minoans had developed some sort of trade network that included the Aeolians by the time of the palace's construction in approximately 1900 B.C. Plates of raw copper that were used by the Minoans as one of their forms of money have been found on the islands of Sicily and Sardinia, indicating a Minoan presence there as well. Substantial amounts of Minoan pottery, dating to approximately 1500 B.C., have been found in Sicily and southern Italy. In southern and eastern Spain, early Spanish pottery has been found that clearly imitates the style and decoration of the Minoan ware. The same distinctive style of Minoan ax that

was found in an archaeological excavation 25 feet beneath the foundation of the palace of Knossos has been found in various places in central Europe. The presence of these artifacts in such diverse locations is the likely result of widespread Minoan trade throughout the entire Mediterranean area.

Ruins of the Minoan palace at Knossos on the island of Crete. "The Minoans were a dark, elegant people of unknown origins," according to the English historian Colin Thubron, "[who] created such a powerful navy that—alone among ancient civilizations—they built their cities without walls."

A freight boat, made of reeds, is towed over a mud flat. In such flimsy vessels, the Egyptians navigated the Nile and even ventured onto the Mediterranean, though they rarely sailed out of sight of land.

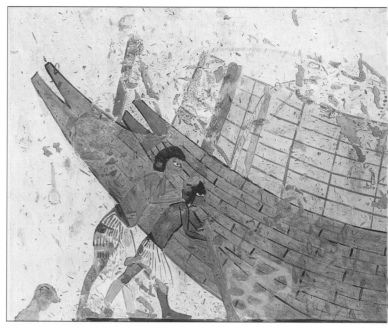

In the 16th century B.C., at the height of the Minoan civilization, a volcano erupted on the island of Santorini, between Crete and Greece. The spectacular palace the Minoans had built on the island was completely buried, and the devastation on the island was complete. Equally terrible consequences were felt throughout the Minoan islands. The force of such a gigantic volcanic blast destroyed crops on the surrounding islands and blanketed the entire area in a fine ash cloud. Earthquakes that followed the eruption toppled the Minoan palaces of Zakro and Mallia on the island of Crete and damaged the palace of Knossos, and many Minoan cities and settlements were abandoned, never to be rebuilt. The entire web of the Minoan civilization was torn apart; starvation and disease came in the wake of the physical destruction of the mighty blast, and social upheaval and possibly foreign invasion from the north followed. The exact sequence of events that followed the eruption is unknown, but

from that moment Minoan influence in world trade and exploration lessened and finally ceased.

Into the void created when the Minoans and Egyptians both ceased to dominate the trade of the ancient world came the Phoenicians. The name *Phoenicians* was given to the peoples who lived along the fertile coastal plain on the far eastern shore of the Mediterranean Sea. Phoenicia referred not to any single country but to a number of independent city-states that dominated the seacoast. The largest of these cities were Tyre, Sidon, Byblos, and Arwad. The major resources of the region were derived from the extensive forests of cedar, juniper, and hardwoods that covered the foothills of the mountains only a few miles from the sea. From the earliest times these lumber products were in high demand by the Egyptians, the Minoans, and other peoples as well. When Solomon, king of the Israelites, was building the temple in Jerusalem, he contracted with Hiram, the king of Tyre, for both lumber and the skilled carpenters to work it.

Despite the fact that it was the Phoenicians who developed the alphabet that we use, they left little written evidence of their history in trade and exploration, even though Phoenicia was famous for its sailors and shipwrights from the earliest times. Phoenician shipwrights were employed in Egypt as early as 2500 B.C. In the Old Testament of the Bible, the prophet Ezekiel compares the city of Tyre to a ship constructed of many fine woods and then notes the far-flung trade of the Phoenicians, both by land and by sea, from Arabia in the East to the Mediterranean in the West.

The Phoenicians not only dispatched commercial and exploratory expeditions; they established permanent colonies at strategic sites for the protection of their trade interests. According to the Bible, Phoenician colonies extended from Ophir, which was probably located in southern Arabia and was famous for its gold, ivory, apes, and peacocks, to Tarshish, a name used to designate the silver mining regions of southern Spain. The Phoenicians established a colony at Gades, outside the Strait of Gibraltar on the coast of Spain, in 1110 B.C.; another at Utica, in Libya on the African coast, in 1101 B.C.; and colonized Sardinia sometime during the 9th century B.C.

Dido, the daughter of the king of Tyre, has traditionally been credited with founding Carthage, near Utica on the Libyan shores of the Mediterranean, in 814 B.C. Over the next 500 years, Carthage and the Phoenicians dominated the trade routes of the Mediterranean world. The farthest documented westward extent of Phoenician colonization was Mogador, on the Atlantic coast of Morocco, and the mouth of the Mondego River in Portugal.

The Phoenicians also ventured far beyond the Mediterranean, in the process accomplishing several of the most daring explorations of ancient history. Foremost among these was the circumnavigation of the continent of Africa from east to west, an adventure recounted in 450 B.C., 150 years after it occurred, by Herodotus:

For Libya [a name often used by the ancients to refer
to all of Africa] furnishes proofs about itself that it is
surrounded by sea, except so much of it as borders
upon Asia; and this fact was shown by Necho, king of
the Egyptians, first of all those about whom we have
knowledge. For when he stopped digging the canal
which stretches from the Nile to the Arabian Gulf
he sent forth Phoenician men in ships, ordering
them to sail back between the Pillars of Heracles
(Strait of Gibraltar) until they came to the Northern
Sea (Mediterranean) and thus to Egypt. The Phoenicians therefore setting forth from the Red Sea sailed
in the Southern Sea (Arabian Sea and Indian Ocean)
and whenever autumn came, they each time put
ashore and sowed the land wherever they might be in
Libya as they voyaged, and awaited the reaping time;
having then reaped the corn they set sail, so that after
the passing of two years they doubled the Pillars of
Heracles in the third year and came to Egypt. And
they told things believable perhaps for others but
unbelievable for me, namely that in sailing round
Libya they had the sun on the right hand. Thus was
Libya known for the first time.

Though Herodotus's sources for this exploit, which he first
heard of while traveling in Egypt, are unknown, and though
no evidence to support it has been found anywhere in
Africa, it is confirmed in its likely truthfulness by a detail
that seemed fantastic to the ancients (and indeed to
Herodotus himself, who discounted the story for precisely
this reason)—the apparent changed location of the sun in
the sky. A ship sailing west in the waters of the Southern
Hemisphere would indeed have the midday sun to its
right—that is, to the north. Herodotus himself believed the
story and cited it as evidence that the waters of the Atlantic
and Indian oceans met at some point, an accurate theory
that was discounted by succeeding generations of
Europeans until the Portuguese explorer Bartholomeu
Dias rounded Africa from the west in the 15th century.

Modern scholars who credit Herodotus's account offer a reconstruction of the Phoenician voyage something like the following:

Necho II, who ruled Egypt from 609 to 593 B.C., was interested in developing new trade routes outside the control of the Phoenicians, who exercised a virtual monopoly on the ports and trade routes of the Mediterranean. The Egyptians were especially interested in gaining direct access to the trade in Spanish silver, and Necho wished to discover a route to Spain that did not involve sailing the Mediterranean, which had become something of a Phoenician lake. If indeed, as the ancients believed, a river of ocean surrounded the continents, and if Africa was, as

This 14th-century-B.C. mural depicts an Egyptian royal ship. Increased commerce with other lands of the Mediterranean both made possible and necessitated the construction of more complex sea vessels; one of the prime objects of Egyptian trade was cedarwood with which to construct ever larger vessels for ever more ambitious sea voyages.

some believed, not very large, it might be a small matter to sail completely around Africa in order to reach Spain without violating the territory claimed by the Phoenicians.

So, Necho II hired some Phoenician sailors and provided them with the ships and equipment that they needed. Their ships probably set sail from the Red Sea ports of Suez or Kosseir in late November and fought against northeast winds and currents as far south as Cape Gaurdafui, Africa's easternmost point. Beyond the so-called Horn of Africa, as monsoon winds and currents carried the journeyers ever southward, it became alarmingly apparent to the Phoenicians that Africa was far larger than anyone had assumed. Every day, the coast of Africa stretched away to the horizon from the right side of the ship; every night, the North Star and the constellation of the Great Bear, by which the Phoenicians navigated, sank closer to the horizon and finally disappeared from sight as the ships crossed the equator. Even the sun seemed to move from its familiar place in the sky, crossing to the north of the ship at noon from its customary position to the south, where the sailors were used to finding it in the northern latitudes of the Mediterranean.

The farther south the intrepid Phoenicians traveled, the farther north journeyed the sun. By the time the ships finally rounded the southern tip of Africa, the sun at noon would be more than halfway to the northern horizon, and the Phoenician explorers must no doubt have been gripped by the fear that if they continued to the south the sun would completely disappear. Such fears appear ridiculous to moderns, who understand that the earth is a globe and that the sun really does not move but remains directly over the equator; it is only the relative location of the viewer that changes the apparent position of the sun in the sky. But to those, like the Phoenicians, who regarded the world as a flat saucer, the prospect was genuinely terrifying.

Finally, the swift Mozambique current funneled the voyagers between Africa and the island of Madagascar, and they rounded the Cape of Good Hope (so named by the royal patron of the Portuguese explorers who doubled it, going in the opposite direction, 2,000 years later) and proceeded due west, through some of the heaviest and most stormy seas in the world, with the help of the Agulhas current.

Once round the cape, the Phoenicians would have concluded that their initial suspicions about the shape of Africa—that it was in essence a peninsula, albeit one much huger than they had surmised—were true. It would now have been April or May, autumn in the Southern Hemisphere, and the Phoenicians likely went ashore to build

Egyptian trading vessels could sail with the wind or be oared against it. Herodotus described Egyptian shipbuilding methods: "The Nile boats used for carrying freight are built of wood . . . . They cut short planks, about three feet long . . . and the method of construction is to lay them together like bricks and fasten them with long spikes set close together."

houses to shelter them through the coming winter and sow winter wheat to sustain them for the remainder of their voyage. In November, the crops were harvested, and the Phoenicians set sail once more.

Pushed north by the helpful Benguela current and a favorable south wind, the Phoenicians must have been encouraged by the seeming southerly movement of the sun, which would have been higher in the sky each day at noon, until, at the mouth of the Niger River, near the equator, it seemed to pass directly overhead. The Great Bear and the North Star reappeared at night; once the Phoenicians reached the great western hump of the African continent at the Gulf of Guinea, it became necessary to row against the adverse winds and calms that frequent the area.

In November, the Phoenicians put in to shore again, somewhere on the coast of Morocco, and planted crops for the year ahead. After harvest in June, they put out to sea for the last time, entered the Mediterranean through the Strait of Gibraltar, and made their way back to the Nile on the waters of that familiar sea.

The Phoenicians braved the Atlantic in other directions as well. About 100 years after the circumnavigation of Africa, the Phoenicians sent an expedition, probably a trading mission, to the North Atlantic under the direction of a Carthaginian named Himilco. Their aim was to secure more direct access to the trade in tin (useful in the production of bronze weapons), which was mined in England. After a four-month absence, Himilco returned to Phoenicia with tales of an ocean filled with inquisitive sea monsters, entangling weeds, and dangerous currents––not at all like the peaceful Mediterranean.

At about the same time, Carthage sent a colonizing expedition south down the Atlantic coast of West Africa. Upon his return, the captain of the voyage, a man named Hanno, posted his account of the improbable journey on the doors of the Temple of Moloch in Carthage for all to admire.

According to Hanno, the expedition consisted of 60 large ships of 50 oars, carrying 30,000 men and women as well as food, livestock, and equipment to establish the various new Carthaginian settlements. Two days' sailing past the Strait of Gibraltar, the Carthaginian colonizers stopped and founded their first settlement, which they called Thymiaterium, along the coast of present-day Morocco. They then sailed westward and established a temple dedicated to Poseidon on a densely wooded promontory that opened onto the Atlantic Ocean. Farther south, after they passed the marshes at the mouth of the Tensift River in western Morocco, the sailors could see elephants and multitudes of other grazing beasts as well as the peaks of the Atlas Mountains in the background.

They then established a series of towns that they named Carian Fort (present-day Essaouira), Gutta, Acra (present-day Agadir), Melitta, and Arambys. Near the Lixus River, they put ashore to visit with nomadic shepherds who kept their flocks on the river's banks. Some of these Lixites were taken aboard as guides and interpreters for the rest of the journey.

The lands beyond the Lixus were inhabited by wild beasts and an inhospitable people the Carthaginians called Ethiopians; the highlands behind the coastal plain were said to be inhabited by a freakish race of men, the Troglodytes, who lived in caves and were said by the Lixites to run faster than horses. Beginning here, the expedition sailed along the western reaches of the Sahara Desert, where it reaches the ocean. Hanno and the Carthaginians founded another outpost at Herne Island, just north of the Tropic of Cancer, before continuing southward.

Once, as they tried to land, they were driven off by swarms of wild men in animal skins who attacked them with rocks, and they found the mouth of the Senegal River filled with crocodiles and hippopotamuses. Beyond the Senegal, the Ethiopians spoke a language even the Lixite interpreters could not understand. At Cape Verde, the westernmost point of Africa, the explorers anchored in a harbor surrounded by forests of fragrant trees; farther on, they anchored in a great gulf, which the Lixite interpreters called the West Horn and was most likely modern-day Bissagos Bay, off the coast of Guinea. The explorers decided to go ashore on a small island within the gulf, but they grew wary at nightfall when they saw, within the deep forest that surrounded them, a multitude of small fires being kindled, and the noise of pipes and cymbals and the din of tom-toms started to sound through the trees. The frightened Carthaginians decided to spend the night aboard their ships, and they left the area the next day.

Even stranger sights were in store; according to Hanno, "for the next several days the expedition coasted along a

The Minoan civilization was given its name by Arthur Evans, a British archaeologist, who derived it from an ancient Greek myth about a Cretan king named Minos, who built an elaborate structure—the labyrinth—to house a fantastic creature, half man and half bull, known as the minotaur. Images of bulls were discovered on many of the artifacts recovered from the ruins at Knossos.

country with a fragrant smoke of blazing timber, from which streams of fire plunged into the sea. The land was unapproachable for the heat. So we sailed away in fear, and in four days' journey saw the land ablaze at night. In the center a leaping flame towered above the others and appeared to reach the stars. This was the highest mountain which we saw: it was called the Chariot of the Gods."

Later explorers of the area reported seeing these same awe-inspiring sights; the Chariot of the Gods was probably Mount Kakulima in Sierra Leone, and the conflagrations were grass fires that swept the plains unchecked.

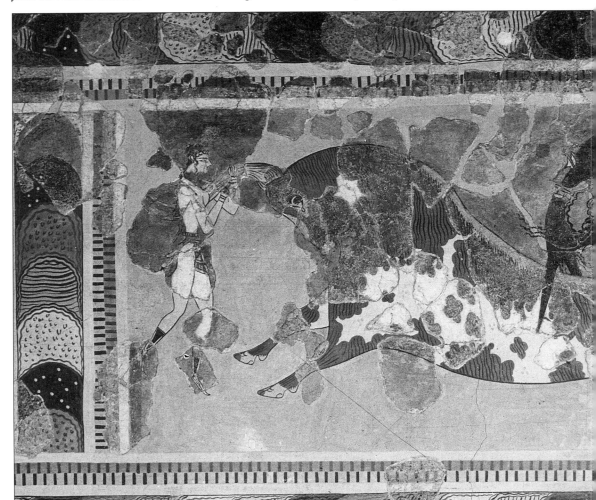

In a gulf the explorers called the Southern Horn (most
likely modern-day Sherbo Sound), the Carthaginians
explored an island that they said was populated by a
tribe of wild people with hairy bodies. Their interpreters
told them that these people were called gorillas. When
the Carthaginians attempted to capture some of these
"people," the gorillas scampered up some steep rocks and
pelted their pursuers with stones. Nevertheless, the explorers succeeded in capturing three of them, whose skins
they brought back with them to Carthage. In all likelihood
the "wild people" were actually chimpanzees rather than
gorillas.

A bas relief of a Phoenician ship at sail. The Phoenicians were the foremost seafaring merchants of the ancient world. The Old Testament prophet Isaiah described the Phoenician metropolis of Tyre as "the crowning city, whose merchants are princes, whose traffickers are the honorable of the earth."

At this point, Hanno called a halt to the expedition due to a lack of provisions, and the explorers returned to Carthage in triumph. The explorers had sailed more than 3,000 miles, to within eight degrees of the equator; in a single summer, Hanno had discovered and explored more of the West African coast than the sailors of the late Middle Ages did in 150 years. The Carthaginians continued to explore and trade along the coast of Africa until approximately 146 B.C., but after Carthage's fall in that year maritime trade with Africa all but ceased. The Greeks and the Romans developed other trade networks, and the magnificent achievement of Hanno and his explorers was little more than a dim memory to the civilized West until the bold seafaring men of Prince Henry the Navigator of Portugal duplicated and then bettered his feat in the 15th century.

The Phoenicians were the master traders and explorers of the ancient world for almost 1,000 years. Because they were a secretive people, jealously guarding their geographic and trade secrets, most of what is known about them comes from their various economic and political rivals, the foremost of whom were the Greeks. Though it was the Phoenicians who created the alphabet, it was the Greeks who used it to immortalize their own achievements.

Exploring the World of the Greeks

When the volcano on Santorini exploded and started the chain of events that resulted in the destruction of the Minoan civilization, the southern mainland of Greece was inhabited, among others, by a race of Indo-Europeans called the Mycenaeans, the first known speakers of the Greek language and rivals of the Minoans. By 1700 B.C., these Mycenaeans were digging deep burial shafts in the ground and burying their royal dead with artifacts of gold, crystal, and jewelry of semiprecious stones, such as lapis lazuli—indications that the Mycenaeans, too, maintained an extensive trade network in the Mediterranean. As the Minoan civilization weakened, the Mycenaeans grew stronger and took over various Minoan outposts and trade routes. By 1400 B.C., Knossos, capital city of Crete, was under Mycenaean control. Mycenaean supremacy was short-lived, however; by 1200 B.C. Greek-speaking tribes from the north had overrun Mycenae, the capital city of the Mycenaeans; several large Mycenaean cities had been burned; and most of the major Mycenaean population centers had been deserted.

Most of the culture of the Mycenaeans disappeared with their civilization. Lost as well were the sailing and trade routes the Mycenaeans had inherited from the Minoans. For several hundred years after the fall of the Mycenaeans

King Cyrus the Great of Persia united much of the Middle East and Central Asia under his reign.

these new Greeks—among them Achaeans, Ionians, Aeolians, and Dorians—traveled little in the Mediterranean, and the various Minoan and Mycenaean outposts were forgotten. During this time the Phoenicians were the masters of the Mediterranean, and they jealously guarded their trade monopolies throughout the region.

But beginning in about 900 B.C., the Phoenicians came under increased pressure from the Babylonian and the Persian empires. Put constantly on the defensive, the Phoenician city-states were unable to support their foreign colonies or engage in further territorial expansion. The Greeks used this historical opportunity to colonize the entire Black Sea area as well as much of the Mediterranean and the Atlantic.

According to Greek legend, it was the Thessalonian prince Jason—the same who according to myth won the

Much Greek mythology, literature, and artwork celebrates the exploits of various travelers, such as this piece of pottery depicting one of the many adventures of Odysseus, protagonist of Homer's Odyssey, *as he returned from the Trojan War.*

famed Golden Fleece—who first made his way into the Black Sea and explored the southern coast as far as the Caucasus Mountains. More likely, it was the Carians, hardy seafaring Greeks living in the farthest southwest corner of modern-day Turkey, who were the first to penetrate the Black Sea and begin to establish colonies along its coast. The presence of early Greek pottery in the ruins of these colonies dates the earliest of these settlements to about 1200 B.C., around the time of the Greek conquest of the city of Troy, which forms the subject of one of the greatest works of Greek literature, *The Iliad.* Just as the myths and legends surrounding the fall of Troy were demonstrated to have had a basis in real life (as proved by 19th-century archaeological excavations), so, too, the myth of the Golden Fleece has an actual basis. The first explorers of the Black Sea reported that the inhabitants of the Caucasus Mountains used the fleece of sheep to trap flecks of gold from the swift mountain streams of their homeland.

At first, the Greeks searched along the Black Sea for new fishing grounds and access to the raw metals that were mined in the surrounding mountains and rivers, but soon they also began trading for the wheat that was grown to the north in the present-day Ukraine. Their settlements in the area gave the Greeks a virtual monopoly on the Black Sea trade; though there were occasional battles between rival Greek city-states for a particular site or trading partner, on the whole the Greeks expanded into the Black Sea in peace. They would maintain a virtual trade monopoly there until the rise of the Roman Empire some 500 years later.

By 800 B.C. the Greeks were also exploring new commercial possibilities in the Mediterranean. Initially, it was most likely the search for new fishing grounds that served as the impetus for Greek expansion in the Mediterranean, just as it had inspired the exploration and colonization of the Black Sea. As soon as Greek fishermen would report the location of a new harbor, traders and merchants would follow to open new markets. The presence of Greek "geometric" pottery dates the foundation of Cumae, near Naples on the west coast of Italy, to around 800 B.C. The Greeks founded a colony, Naxos, on Sicily in 735 B.C. Sicily and Italy had largely been ignored by the Phoenicians, and the Greek colonies grew unobstructed there.

Greek exploration in the western reaches of the Mediterranean occurred first by accident. Around 650 B.C., according to the tradition of the ancient Greek legend, a Greek merchant named Colaeus, from the town of Samos, was sailing from Platea to Egypt, when a storm and easterly winds drove him westward all the way through the Strait of Gibraltar and into the Atlantic Ocean. He was forced to land at the mouth of the Guadalquivir River, the site of the settlement of Tartessus, the main depot for the rich silver trade of the region. The location of Tartessus had been one of the most closely guarded trade secrets of the Phoenicians for centuries, for it was the Tartessians who had established a sea route to the tin mines of Britain.

Colaeus bartered for a rich cargo of silver and, eluding the Phoenicians for a second time, passed back through the Strait of Gibraltar and returned to Samos, where his cargo made him a very wealthy man. His good luck inspired other Greek entrepreneurs and mariners to follow in his wake, to the extent that the entire economy of the neighboring city of Phocaea became virtually dependent on the Spanish trade. Using warships rather than merchantmen, and relying on municipal financing rather than individual initiative, Phocaea established an extensive network of colonies on Mediterranean islands along the trade routes to Spain. From the Greek settlements in Sicily or on the island of Ischia in the Bay of Naples, the Phocaean ships sailed past the Balearic Islands to Sardinia. From Sardinia they passed to the islands of Mallorca and Menorca and then to the island of Iviza. From Iviza, the Phocaean ships steered for Puenta de Yfach, a narrow promontory on the southeast Spanish coast, and then, keeping the coast of Spain to

This illustration from a medieval German illuminated manuscript depicts Greek ships laying siege to Troy. Because of the so-called Great Interruption of geographic knowledge in Europe, medieval Europeans often looked to the ancients for geographic information. In modern times, archaeological research has revealed that many of the Greek legends and myths were rooted in historical truths.

starboard as they skirted its southern face, they headed for their trading settlement at Maenace, just inside the Strait of Gibraltar.

From these outposts, the Phocaean explorers then ventured north and explored the Gulf of Lyons and the Mediterranean coast of France and Italy. When a preliminary expedition to the mouth of the Rhône River returned to Phocaea with glowing reports of the natural beauties of the area, a second expedition was sent under the command of two men, Simus and Protis, who were instructed to

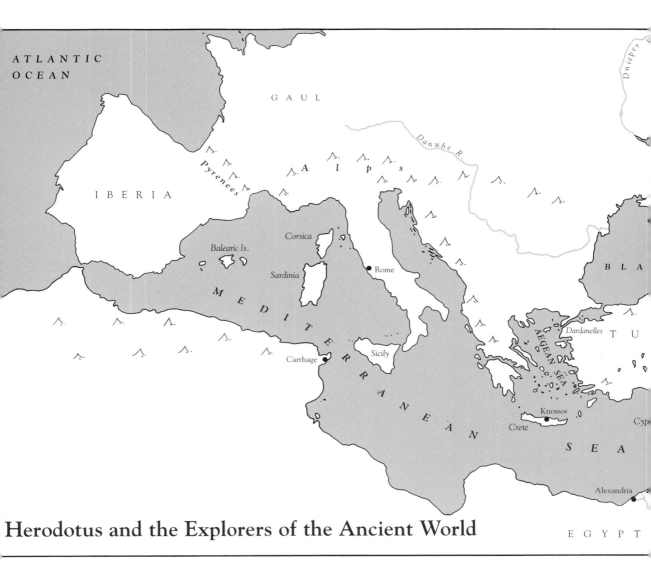

Herodotus and the Explorers of the Ancient World

The regions visited by the explorers of the ancient world included most of the lands abutting the Mediterranean as well as the realms of the Middle East and Central Asia.

solicit the friendship of the local ruler, Nanus, and gain permission to found a new settlement.

As it happened, King Nanus was just then preparing to marry off his daughter, Gyptis. According to custom, Gyptis was to choose her husband from the guests her father invited to the wedding feast and marry him on the spot. At the wedding party, Gyptis chose one of the newcomers—Protis—to be her husband, and the Greeks received per-

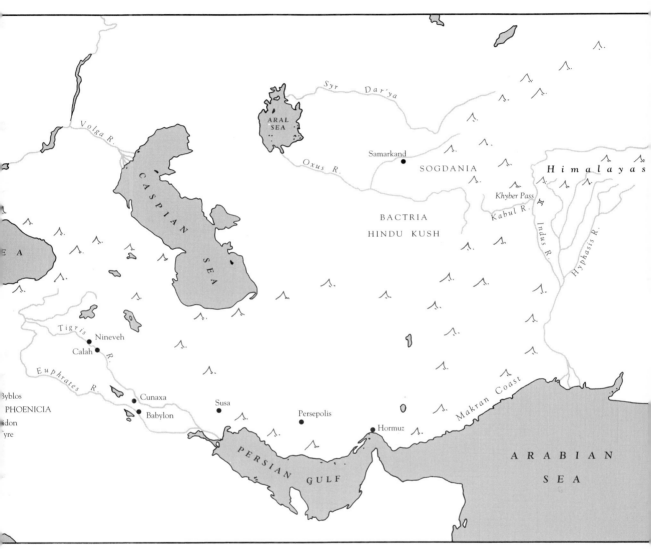

mission for their settlement from Nanus. Thus was the
Greek colony of Massilia (present-day Marseilles, France's
oldest city) founded. Massilia quickly grew from a small
fishing hamlet to a major Greek city of the ancient world,
from which the Phocaean explorers sailed east and west
along the coasts of Italy, France, and Spain. By 500 B.C. a
belt of Phocaean settlements stretched along the Mediterranean coast from Nice in France to Alicante in Spain,

Wood logs are loaded aboard Phoenician ships for transport back to their home ports. Wood for shipbuilding was a highly sought after commodity in the ancient world, but the most desirable natural resources were precious metals and gems. Over the course of history, the search for natural resources and other desirable economic commodities has been the primary motivation behind most exploration.

but the Phoenicians soon acted to reexert their dominance of the silver trade. The Phoenicians destroyed Tartessus and systematically drove the Greeks from the Spanish coast, the Balearic Islands, and Sardinia, though Massilia was spared.

One result was that by 450 B.C. knowledge of the western Mediterranean had disappeared from Greek culture. Herodotus wrote about the Phoenician circumnavigation of Africa, but he did not know the geography of the Greek settlements in Spain.

By this time wars of empire had exhausted the Phoenician cities of the Levant, and Carthage, on the northern coast of Africa near the site of present-day Tunis in Tunisia, had become the leading Phoenician power. Unless preoccupied with war or internal problems, Carthage maintained a stranglehold on the commerce of the western Mediterranean for hundreds of years, allowing no ships of a rival power to pass through the Strait of Gibraltar.

Despite the Carthaginian vigilance, around 310 B.C. an enterprising Greek merchant named Pytheas slipped through the strait in order to open direct trade in tin with the miners of the British Isles. Though little is known of Pytheas, an account of his journey, presumed to be first-hand, has survived; it indicates that, at the very least, he was a competent scientist by the standards of the day and a skilled astronomer. During the voyage, he observed that the Pole Star was not situated at true north, measured the tides, determined the latitude of his home port of Marseilles to within a few minutes of the correct figure, and computed

This ancient bas relief shows, at top left, a Greek phalanx ready for battle. The discipline of the Greeks in battle became legend throughout the ancient world.

the latitudes of places that another Greek, Hipparchus, later used to create one of the first known maps of the world.

Pytheas's voyage took him from Marseilles to Cádiz, a port on the Atlantic on the southwest coast of Spain, and then north along the western Iberian coast. He hugged the shore traveling east and then north along the Bay of Biscay before skirting the coast of Brittany west to Ushant Island. From Brittany, Pytheas crossed the English Channel to Britain, where he made shore at Land's End. Pytheas described the miners of Cornwall as ingenious and hard-working and the tin mines of Cornwall as an elaborate commercial enterprise, involving smelting and transportation to market as well as the digging of ore. The inhabitants of Britain, he wrote, were "far removed from the cunning and knavishness of modern man. Their diet is inexpensive and quite different from the luxury that is born of wealth. The island is thickly populated, and has an extremely chilly climate, as one would expect in a sub-Arctic region. It has many kings and potentates, who live for the most part in a state of mutual peace."

Metalwork on a Scythian sword depicts the Greeks and Persians in battle. The clash of Greek civilization with those of the East was the dominant theme of Herodotus's Histories.

From Land's End, Pytheas sailed completely around the British Isles. He noted in his journal that the islands were triangular in shape, like Sicily, and he provided measurements of the three sides that were twice their actual size but accurate in proportion. In the north, above Scotland, he challenged seas running "80 cubits" high, a reference to the gales of Pentland Firth, where the winds and tides regularly whip the waves to heights of 60 feet or more, with the spray rising another 100 feet above that.

Though he never put ashore on Ireland, Pytheas probably caught a glimpse of the Emerald Isle, and it was in all likelihood Pytheas who provided the information about Ireland's location that was used by the Greek geographer Eratosthenes for his famous map of the world.

Pytheas also reported on another island, one that future explorers and geographers had much more difficulty locating. According to the Greek explorer, the northernmost of the British Isles was a body of land named Thule, which lay six days' sail north of Britain. On Thule, said brave Pytheas, to the amazement of his ancient readers, the midsummer night was only two to three hours long, and the midsummer

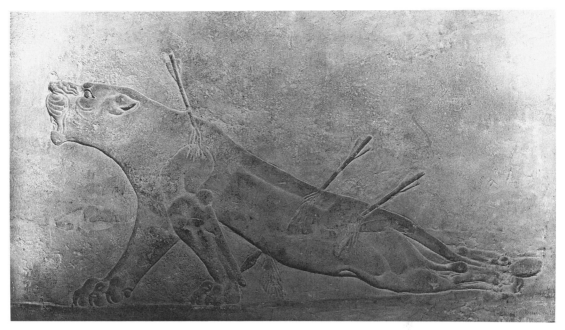

Wild beasts, of a kind not known in the Greek homelands, were just some of the strange sights seen by the Ten Thousand in the course of their retreat through the Persian Empire.

sun rose only two-thirds of the way above the horizon. A permanent fog filled the air, and the climate was too cold to raise crops or to keep cattle. The inhabitants lived on wild berries and millet. Honey was plentiful and used to make mead, a potent alcoholic beverage. Pytheas admitted that all of his information about Thule had been gathered secondhand; in all likelihood he was describing Norway on the Scandinavian Peninsula. Some hardy souls were already sailing directly between Scotland and Scandinavia at the time, and Pytheas no doubt discussed with Scottish sailors the sea route north and what was to be found at its conclusion.

After circumnavigating the British Isles, Pytheas recrossed the English Channel and continued to explore the Atlantic Coast of Europe to the northeast, sailing, he claimed, "beyond the Rhine to Scythia." His most noteworthy discovery en route was an island, which he called Abalus, that sat in the mouth of a broad river, the Elbe, where it emptied into the sea. On Abalus, the natives told him, amber, which was much valued in the ancient world for decorative and ornamental purposes, was washed by the tides onto the shore, where it was gathered by the inhabitants for use as fuel. The best modern reconstruction of his trip places the amber island at Heligoland (on the North Sea in present-day Germany, near its border with Denmark), which later became the depot for much of the trade in the precious petrified jewel. With his ships laden with tin from Great Britain and amber from the northern forests, Pytheas returned home. Though his 7,000-mile voyage had been a remarkable success, the Greeks were unable to maintain direct trade contact with Britain or the amber coast along the North Sea. The Carthaginians again closed the Strait of Gibraltar and prevented all travel outside of the Mediterranean Sea, and Pytheas's Thule and the island of amber entered into the realm of mythology.

The thriving commerce of the Middle East attracted many invaders, but only the Greeks succeeded in defeating the Persian Empire.

At the same time that the Greeks were exploring the Mediterranean and the Black seas, their attention was focused as well on the East and the continent of Asia. While the Greek city-states were producing fine soldiers, immortal literature, and the world's first democracy, the various lands and peoples of the Near East were being consolidated into vast empires under the direction of a powerful, despotic ruler.

The early Eastern empires—those of the Babylonians and the Assyrians—never extended as far as the Mediterranean coast and therefore had little direct effect on the emerging Greek city-states, but in the 7th century B.C., a Lydian king, Gyges, subdued the Greek cities in Asia Minor and made them pay a regular tribute to him for their freedom. In 546 B.C., the last of the Lydian kings, Croesus,

Through all the long centuries, these stone figures, found in an archaelogical dig in present-day Iran, have silently contemplated the lost grandeur of the Persian Empire.

was defeated by Cyrus the Great, the emperor of the Persians, who had already combined the kingdoms of Persia, Media, and Assyria under his dominion and now added Lydia and most of the Greek settlements in Asia Minor to his control. Between 500 and 449 B.C., the comparatively small Greek city-states held off several separate Persian invasions, a heroic struggle that formed the basis of Herodotus's *Histories*.

The fanatical courage and discipline of Greece's fighting men—in one of their most legendary feats, 300 Greeks held off 150,000 Persians at a small mountain pass known as Thermopylae for six days—made them the most admired soldiers in the world. Many of them hired out as mercenaries to foreign powers, even, during the infrequent periods of peace between the two rivals, in the army of the Persian emperors. The experience of one such band of Greek mercenaries, known as the Ten Thousand, constitutes one of the first documented episodes of European exploration of the continent of Asia as well as one of the greatest marches in military history.

The Ten Thousand were hired in 401 B.C. by Cyrus, satrap (provincial governor) of Lydia, a dominion of the Persian Empire. Ostensibly, the Ten Thousand were to help Cyrus quell a rebellion in the mountainous region of Pisidia (on the Mediterranean in present-day southern Turkey). Cyrus kept his real intentions from the Ten Thousand, however; he was himself planning a rebellion against his brother Artaxerxes, the emperor.

From Sardis, a small city on the Aegean, the Ten Thousand, supplemented by Persian warriors loyal to Cyrus, marched east toward Pisidia, following a system of valleys and keeping the Taurus Mountains—the stronghold of the rebels—always to their south. When Cyrus's army finally did enter the mountains, it purposely did not engage the rebels, and when the army emerged at Tarsus, the Greeks began to suspect that they had been misled. Cyrus persuaded them nonetheless to follow him farther east to the Euphrates River, where he was forced to reveal to the Ten Thousand their true destination and mission: the capital city of Babylon and the overthrow of Artaxerxes.

Their reluctance overcome by Cyrus's promises of fabulous treasures and the discipline imposed by the officer Clearchus, the Ten Thousand crossed the Euphrates in August of 401 B.C. and marched southeast along the banks of the river, which constituted, in effect, the main highway to the capital and the waiting Artaxerxes. Their route took them through the Arabian Desert, where they encountered many animals unknown to them—wild asses, gazelles, ostriches, and others—and finally to Cunaxa, in Babylonia, where Artaxerxes' huge army easily defeated them in battle.

With Cyrus killed in battle, Clearchus took command of the Ten Thousand, and he accepted the offer made by Tissaphernes, the greatest of the Persian generals, to escort their force safely out of the Persian Empire. The Ten Thousand now marched north, on the east bank of the Tigris, to and then beyond the ruins of the old Mesopotamian cities of Nineveh and Calah, where, after kidnapping and killing Clearchus and the other Persian commanders, Tissaphernes and the Persian escort abandoned the Greeks to their own devices. Beyond lay the wild, mountainous, unknown regions of Kurdistan and Armenia; behind lay 1,500 hostile miles, controlled by their enemies, between them and the sea.

At this point Xenophon, a disciple of the philosopher Socrates, was elected by his fellows to lead. After listening to conflicting advice "from the men who claimed to know the way in every direction," Xenophon decided to take his men into the mountains, in the belief that by following the region's rivers north they would reach the Black Sea. It was now winter, and the weary Greeks were traversing, unaided by charts, reliable information, or navigational instruments, under frequent attack by Kurdish tribesmen,

The palace walls at Persepolis, administrative capital of the Persian Empire. Alexander the Great ordered the royal palace at Persepolis destroyed "during a drinking bout when he was no longer in control of his wits," according to the Greek historian Diodorus.

some of the most rugged terrain in the world. The cold and snow claimed many; hunger, many more; they left behind on the mountain paths "those whose eyes had been blinded by snow, and those whose toes had been rotted off by the cold." Only the generosity of some Armenian tribespeople, who sheltered the Greeks in the rock caves where they endured the region's fierce winters, kept the Ten Thousand from perishing. After a heartbreaking week of travel eastward along the Araxes River, in the mistaken belief that it would ultimately bend north, what remained of the Ten Thousand, by following northward-flowing watercourses, at last, from the slopes of Mount Thechus, were able to cry out joyfully, "Thalassa! Thalassa!" (The Sea! The Sea!). The Greek settlement of Trapezus, on the Black Sea, was just a few days' march away.

The valiant retreat of the Ten Thousand, chronicled by Xenophon, in his famous *Anabasis* (*The Up March*), inspired Greek dreams of making the Persian Empire their own. The information gained by Xenophon and his men in their marches across the outer reaches of the empire demonstrated that a proper fighting force could conceivably challenge the Persians in their homeland. Philip, king of Macedon, who by his conquest of the city-states of Athens and Thebes in 338 B.C. brought all of Greece under his sway, was one of those who dreamed of launching just such an invasion, but it was left to his son Alexander, to be known ultimately as the Great, to make that vision a reality.

Riding Bucephalus, his powerful, faithful charger, Alexander the Great leads his force into battle against the Persians.

Alexander the Great's decision to submit to the will of the gods and the men of his army and return to Greece from India in July of 325 B.C. did not mark the end of his and his army's exploration of the known world. Although his men had experienced enough adventure for one lifetime, he had not, and he hoped to use his retreat to pioneer a sea route from the mouth of the Indus River to the Euphrates. At the mouth of the Indus, he split his army in three. One group, numbering between 3,000 and 5,000 men, was to

The further adventures of Alexander the Great: His army defeats an enemy force by heating huge copper balls on which the enemy's war elephants burn their trunks; from a medieval German manuscript.

sail under the command of his admiral, Nearchus, through the Arabian Sea to the mouth of the Euphrates at the head of the Persian Gulf. The largest contingent, about 85,000 men, women, and children, was to march under Alexander himself along the coastline of the Arabian Sea toward the Euphrates. A smaller group, under Craterus and consisting mostly of the sick and wounded and the army's captured contingent of war elephants, was to tramp a similar course, but farther inland.

Alexander's march along the Makran Coast of present-day Pakistan and Iran was a hellish ordeal. The desert and mountain landscape was barren, devoid of sources of food or water, forcing the army to slaughter its pack animals and eat them; the blasting heat allowed the army to move only at night. Sixty thousand people perished during that grimmest of marches, which ended at Salmous, where Alexander and the survivors were reunited with Craterus, whose journey had been comparatively uneventful.

Though plagued by the same problems of hunger and thirst as Alexander, Nearchus and his men survived their voyage in much better shape. Taking advantage of the northwest monsoons, his more than 100 ships were sped along the coast, although their sailors were forced to anchor them and go ashore each day in search of food and fresh water. Along the Iranian coast, such excursions were

Alexander lays siege to a city; from a medieval German manuscript.

In one of the more fanciful episodes from the Alexander legends, he and his men are attacked by hippopotamuses—which are rendered in this medieval German illustration as looking much like sea horses—as they ford a river.

made perilous by the presence of people that the Greeks called "turtle-eaters," men wild in appearance, with long hair, dressed in the skins of animals and porpoises and armed with sticks. According to Strabo, a Greek geographer who recounted Nearchus's adventures more than 300 years later, the turtle-eaters kept their fingernails long and used them like claws to kill fish and cut wood. They ate the flesh of turtles and used their shells as the roofs for their huts. At other points, the men of Nearchus's fleet encountered individuals that they deemed the Ichthyophagi, or fish-eaters, who subsisted on fish meal, fed their flocks dried fish, considered bread the greatest of delicacies, and lived in huts fashioned from whale bones.

Not all the exotic sights were confined to the land. In the Arabian Sea off the settlement of Cyiza, Nearchus and his men were amazed to see columns of water being blown upward from the sea as though they were being carried aloft by a whirlwind. To his amazement, Nearchus learned from his guides that the disturbance was caused by huge fish—whales—"who blow the water aloft as they pass through it." In a short time, a pod of whales surfaced, and Nearchus ordered a frontal attack on them as if they were an enemy fleet. As they did in combat, the Greeks raised a battle cry with drums and trumpets as the whales approached. The mariners were then astonished to see the whales dive below the surface, disappear from sight, and resurface far behind their ships, spouting vast columns of water into the air again.

After reuniting with Nearchus and Craterus at Susa, Alexander decided to complete his maritime endeavors by exploring the trade routes to Arabia, the land of exotic woods and spices. Learning a lesson in logistics from Nearchus's difficulties in keeping his huge expedition well supplied, Alexander now sent out a succession of single ships, each crewed by only 30 or so men, each venturing a little farther across the Persian Gulf along the Arabian Peninsula. Using the information he thus gathered, Alexander the Great was laying plans for the establishment of Greek trading posts along the Arabian Peninsula and for a voyage of circumnavigation around Africa when he died on June 10, 323 B.C., probably from the combined effects of fever and debauchery but possibly as a result of being poisoned.

Alexander made much of the known world part of his own empire, but his realm was too far-flung to hold together for long after his death, and as his dominion fragmented, much of the information he had added to the store of available geographic knowledge was lost. In the European consciousness, the remote lands of Asia Minor once again became shrouded in myth and legend—desirable destinations as the source of precious stones and metals and various other commodities, such as silk and spices, highly desired in Europe, but too remote and dangerous, in a world

Alexander's last march constituted a formidable feat of exploration: With engineers and road builders cutting a path before them as they went, 64 mules, wearing golden bells, dragged the golden jewel-encrusted temple that held Alexander's solid-gold coffin across 1,000 miles of unexplored Asia to his final resting place at Alexandria, Egypt.

again fragmented, to be easily reached. It would not be until the rise of another remarkable civilization, also capable of uniting much of the world under its sway, that ancient Europe would again look outward.

The Roman World

By the middle of the 3rd century B.C., Rome, a small city-state on the western coast of the Italian Peninsula, was ready to challenge mighty Carthage for the supremacy of the Mediterranean world. In that year Rome sent troops to aid the city of Messana (present-day Messina), a Greek-speaking city on the island of Sicily that was under siege from the combined forces of the Carthaginians and the Syracusans (Syracuse was a powerful city-state on the east coast of Sicily) under the command of King Hiero II. When the Romans and the Carthaginians clashed at Agrigentum, on Sicily, in 261 B.C., it marked the beginning of the first of the three Punic Wars, as a consequence of which Rome would wrest control of the commerce of the Mediterranean from Carthage and, by extension, take the leading role in the exploration of the ancient world. For the Romans, more than any other people before them, exploration was a function of commerce. "When the Romans explored," wrote the historian Eric Newby, "they did so mostly with the express purpose of enriching in some way the mighty Roman Empire. . . . Romans were motivated by what one historian describes as 'an unmatched love of gain.' "

The First Punic War lasted 20 years and ended when Carthage sued for peace after a great naval battle off the Aegates Islands in 241 B.C. The victory was a costly one for Rome; more than 100,000 Romans died in the fighting, and the prize for their sacrifice—the island of Sicily—was reduced by the warfare to a devastated, deserted wasteland. Unsatisfied with its gain, Rome then invaded the former

At the height of its empire, Rome's influence extended beyond even the farthest reaches of Alexander's realm. The figure at center in this painting from an Egyptian sarcophagus is wearing the garb of a citizen of Rome; beside him stand more commonly seen Egyptian images.

Carthaginian domain of Sardinia, while Carthage, largely through the efforts of its brilliant generals Hamilcar and Hasdrubal, expanded its empire to southern Spain, where a new capital city, Cartagena, which means New Carthage, was founded on the Mediterranean near rich lead, copper, iron, and zinc mines.

When, in 219 B.C., Hannibal, who was destined to become the most renowned of the Carthaginian commanders, conquered the Roman town of Saguntum, which was 200 miles north of Cartagena, the stage was set for the Second Punic War. The Romans sent a delegation to Carthage to demand Hannibal's surrender. The Carthaginians, said Fabius, the leader of the Roman delegation,

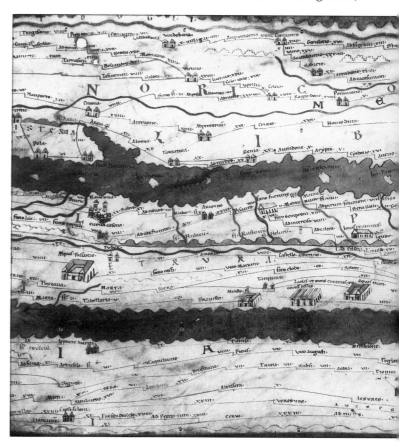

Rome's soldiers, merchants, and engineers extended the boundaries of the known world to include new lands in western Europe and central Asia. Shown here is a detail from the Tabula Peutingeriana, *a medieval rendering of an ancient Roman road map.*

could have either peace or war; which would they choose?
"Whichever you please," came the Carthaginian reply.
"We do not care."

The Romans believed that at this point they held a great
strategic advantage. Since Roman ships now dominated
the Mediterranean, Hannibal and his army were essentially
trapped in Spain on the coast, between the sea and the
hostile Celtic tribesmen of the interior. Carthage dared not
send any more of its army to Hannibal's relief, for fear that
the Roman fleet would intercept the ships carrying its
soldiers before they ever reached Spain. In the meantime,
there was nowhere for Hannibal to go, and Rome could
take its time organizing an expedition of invasion.

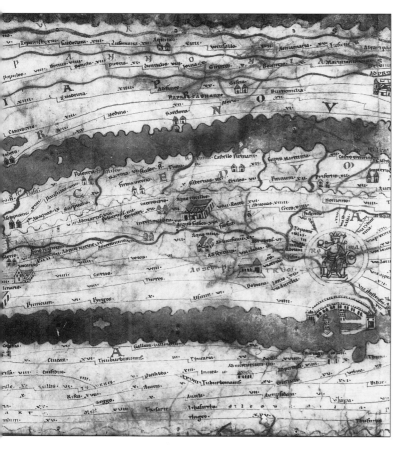

Hannibal's crossing of the Alps with his army of men and war elephants still constitutes one of the most brilliant strategic and command feats in military history.

Hannibal had other ideas, however, and he decided to take his entire army—more than 100,000 men from all parts of the Mediterranean world formerly dominated by the Carthaginians, including Iberians and Celtiberians from Spain, fierce Numidian cavalry from the desert vastness of North Africa, Berber tribesmen from the Atlas Mountains, and 37 war elephants—to Rome by land and lay siege to the city. Such a plan involved taking this entire unwieldy force on a march across more than 1,000 miles of uncharted, hostile wilderness. Numerous rivers and two of the world's major mountain ranges—the Pyrenees and the Alps—blocked their way.

At that time, the European interior was still largely unexplored by the Mediterranean peoples, who regarded it as the realm of a multitude of wild, uncivilized, fearsome people—barbarians, to the Romans. Though several of the continent's large rivers had been navigated by the Greeks of Alexander the Great's time, the interior lands away from the rivers were unknown and decidedly unfriendly.

Interior Europe was divided among a number of independent tribes. The lands that the Romans called Iberia (modern-day Spain and Portugal) were dominated by two major tribes. The Iberians were the oldest inhabitants of the region; the taller and blonder Celts were newcomers who had recently overrun most of western Europe, including the islands of Britain and Ireland. The term *Celts* referred to a number of different tribes, each of whom was ruled by a warrior-king. Many of the lands of present-day France, through some of which Hannibal would have to pass, were controlled by Celtic tribes known as the Gauls. (Gaul was the Roman name for France.) In order to raid northern Italy, the Celts had opened three passes through the Alps; these, along with the longer-established Brenner Pass through which amber and other desirable commodities had reached the Mediterranean from northern Europe, were essentially the only overland links connecting the Italian Peninsula with the European interior.

In the spring of 218 B.C., Hannibal marched his army out of Cartagena and along the Hurcian Plain toward Saguntum, through generally friendly territory occupied by Celtiberians. One hundred miles north of Saguntum, Hannibal and his army forded the Ebro, the mightiest river in Spain, near the town of Tortosa, thereby crossing as well into the domain of several warring Celtic tribes. The Carthaginian army now had to fight its way forward, and its progress was slow and costly. According to the Roman historian Livy, whose life's work was a 142-volume history of his home city, Hannibal "led ninety thousand infantry and twelve thousand cavalry across the Iberus [Ebro]. He then subdued the Ilergetes, the Bargusii, the Austoni, and that part of Lacetania which lies at the foot of the Pyrenees Mountains; and he placed Hanno in command over all the district, that the narrow gorges which connect Spain with Gaul might be under his power." (The Pyrenees separate Spain and France.)

At the cost of 22,000 men who perished in the fighting, Hannibal had opened and secured the northeast coast of Spain between Cartagena and the Pyrenees. The army now marched along the east coast road through the cities of

Another detail from the Tabula Peutingeriana. *The Roman road network set out from Rome in 12 directions and extended to the remotest outposts of the empire.*

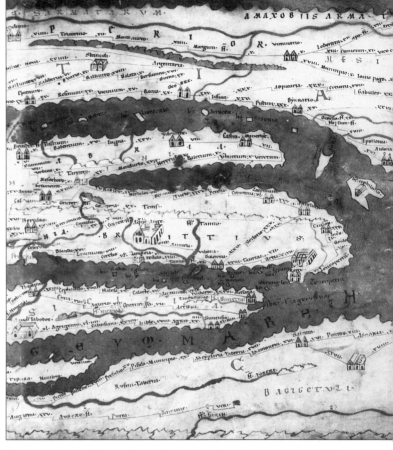

Tarragona and Barcelona, between the mountains and the sea. At Emporion (modern-day Ampurias), a remnant of the old Greek trading empire, the Carthaginians were welcomed, and Hannibal allowed his men to rest and refresh themselves for several days.

The Carthaginians crossed the Pyrenees into Gaul through the wide and gentle pass between Junqueras and Le Perthus and moved toward the Rhône River on the Mediterranean. The cumbersome column of men, animals, and equipment was slowed by numerous shallow, muddy marshes along the Rhône Delta, in which sedge (not unlike the papyrus of the Nile Delta), flamingos, and herds

of wild white horses and cattle were seen. At a broad, flat curve in the Rhône, on the site of present-day Arles, Hannibal decided to cross the river, but on the eastern bank, the Volcae, a Celtic tribe, waited to drive the newcomers away.

Using timber hewn from the thick local forests, the Carthaginians constructed large rafts for the cavalry, which was dispatched far upriver to make its crossing. Meanwhile, each soldier was ordered to fashion his own aquatic conveyance—raft, float, or canoe—from whatever resources were at hand, and with this flotsam and jetsam the huge Carthaginian force crossed the river, reaching the far side just as the Numidian cavalry was dealing a fatal blow to the right flank of the Volcae.

Having attained a beachhead, Hannibal now had to cross his elephants. The Carthaginians built huge rafts, 50 feet wide and 200 feet long, and covered them with dirt to make them look like land. The rafts were then floated out into the river and towed to the far side. Once the elephants realized they were afloat, some of them grew fearful or enraged and began stomping and trumpeting, but most of the pachyderms froze in silent terror at the sight of water all around them. Some upset their crafts and fell into the water, where they either floated or walked ashore. Despite the pandemonium, all of the elephants were safely crossed, though several of the army's mahouts—African keepers and handlers of the beasts—were drowned. This repre-sented a most serious loss to the Carthaginian army, for, then as now, training and handling an elephant is a most delicate task.

Across the Rhône, Hannibal and his troops marched north in search of a route through the Alps. With the aid of Brancus, a local chieftain, the Carthaginians reached the valley of the Drome River, where the watercourse narrows at it flows between high limestone ridges and heavily forested mountains that mark the beginning of the Alps.

Here, at the Gorge de Gas, sheer rock walls stretched upward for more than 800 feet from a bottom wide enough only for the river and a single wagon; all the strategic sites commanding the pass were held by hostile Gauls. For-tunately for the Carthaginians, the Gauls did not believe that anyone would be foolhardy enough to try the gorge at night, and they left their positions unguarded after dark. When night fell, Hannibal, with a small group of select troops, scaled the sheer walls of the gorge and secured control of the most strategic overlooks. Though the Gauls did launch an attack on the richly laden train of supply wagons that trailed behind the main column, for the most part they could do nothing but watch as the Carthaginian army, 60,000 strong, with cavalry and elephants, marched through the pass.

Beyond the Gorge de Gas, the land opened into a high mountain valley, at the far end of which were the last snowy peaks separating the Carthaginians from the Po Valley in Italy. But there were still more stony canyons and gorges, fiercely defended by Gauls, separating the invaders from their destination. Bombarded with rocks and boulders tipped down on them from above, the seven-mile-long Carthaginian column slowed to a crawl in the narrow passes, while ahead Hannibal and his trusted advance guard fought hand-to-hand combat. In one 24-hour period, the army could march no more than four abreast. Twenty-one thousand Carthaginian soldiers died between the crossing of the Rhône and the passage into the high Alps.

In the mountains, cold and hunger became the Carthaginians' greatest enemies. Too weak to continue, men lay down and died on the frosty trails. Others froze to death

This Roman mosaic shows pygmies hunting wild animals along the Nile. The famous Roman games, which were staged in arenas throughout the empire, provided a constant market for wild animals and exotic peoples from Africa.

in their sleep. The horses were slaughtered for food. The great weight of the elephants enabled them to tromp down the snow and gain a secure foothold even on the most precipitous pathways, but many less fortunate soldiers slipped off the icy ridges and fell screaming to their deaths. At the highest elevations, there was not even wood enough for the Carthaginians to build fires at night. Storms raged for days on end, and huge boulders blocked their path. When Hannibal at last descended into the verdant Po Valley, he had scarcely more than 20,000 men at his command. Although he would roam the Italian Peninsula for the next 15 years, thrashing whatever forces Rome sent after him, undone finally only by Carthage's failure to send him reinforcements, none of his victories in Italy constituted as brilliant a feat as his simply getting there. In addition to being one of the greatest military campaigns in history, Hannibal's improbable passage from Cartagena to Italy, across the Pyrenees and Alps, constituted the earliest significant organized exploration of western Europe.

The Romans brought captured pygmies as well as elephants, rhinoceroses, and wild cats from Africa to Rome. The pygmies were used both as animal handlers and as participants in the Roman games.

With their supreme mercantile and military instincts, the Romans quickly saw the advantage of creating a network of carefully maintained and guarded roads that would link Rome and the lands (among others) that Hannibal had traversed—roads that would carry the Roman legions on their many expeditions of exploration and conquest; roads on which precious commodities and resources could be carried to market for barter and sale. By A.D. 69, a latter-day Hannibal could have—as did a huge Roman army that year on its way to quash a revolt in northern Gaul—easily crossed the Alps through the Pass of the Great St. Bernard (one of the original Celtic crossings), 8,111 feet above sea level, in just a few days in the dead of winter, with no undue hardship, along a wide paved road that still exists. For among their other accomplishments, the Romans were exceptional engineers who built roads to unify their far-flung empire, which by the second century A.D. encompassed all of the Italian and Balkan peninsulas, western Europe from present-day Spain and Portugal to France, all of the Middle East including the Levant, Turkey, and many of the lands adjoining the Black Sea, and a wide strip of coastal northern Africa stretching from the Atlantic Ocean to the Red Sea; in short, all of the lands—and more—ever claimed by the Greeks, Carthaginians, Phoenicians, or any of their other predecessors as explorers and conquerors of the ancient world. Lined up end to end, the Roman system of all-weather highways would have stretched 10 times around the world at the equator.

A Roman road was a work of art. The topsoil was shoveled away to a depth of three feet, and the foundation for the new road was leveled. The roadway was laid with small stones, which were then covered with larger, many-sided stones laid so close together that a knife could not be inserted between them. The top stones—when they could be obtained—were of a hard lava that would wear for thousands of years. Roman roads were straight and level, for Roman engineers did not hesitate to tunnel through mountains or to bridge valleys. Every mile, the Romans erected a six-foot cylindrical road marker that provided the distance to Rome and commemorated the emperor responsible for the construction of that particular highway. One such marker erected in A.D. 100 along a Roman road in Yugoslavia reads: "The emperor [Trajan] . . . built this road by cutting through mountains and eliminating the curves."

In many ways, the Romans' system of roads and bridges was their most important weapon in the conquest of Europe. More often than not, the Roman legions were greatly outnumbered in their forays into the European interior, but they had an enormous advantage in their ability to transport men and material quickly and efficiently and to maintain communications with distant outposts.

The Tabula Peutingeriana *mapped Roman roads from Rome as far west as the Atlantic Coast of the Iberian Peninsula, as far north as Gaul (present-day France) and parts of Germany and England, as far south as the Horn of Africa, and as far east as India. This detail shows Roman roads in the Middle East.*

With the Mediterranean and its islands secured by its fleets, Rome was able to devote much of its attention to the conquest and commercial exploitation of the European mainland, especially after the defeat of Hannibal and the ultimate destruction, decades later, of Carthage itself. The Roman emperors focused first on Iberia and Gaul, the lands Hannibal had crossed, which seemed for that reason to pose the greatest potential dangers. Iberia, the richest province, was the first to fall; by 133 B.C. virtually all of the peninsula, with its rich silver mines, belonged to Rome. In conquered territories, the Romans always first built a fort, to secure their conquest, and then a roadway. The Via Augusta, the principal Roman road in Spain, was begun in 120 B.C.; it ran from Massilia along the curve of the seacoast to Ampurias, inland to Saragossa and then to Cartagena. The Via

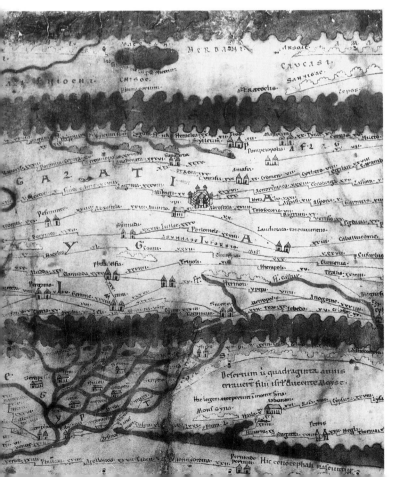

Argenta, or "silver road," the second highway built by the Romans in Spain, ran from Cádiz inland to Italica along the Guadalquivir River and then overland to Merida. In a short time, Roman roads crisscrossed the entire peninsula; by the 3rd century A.D. the Romans had constructed 34 roads in Spain. Along these highways traveled Roman soldiers, merchants, and settlers who brought the Roman laws, customs, and language.

The first Roman road through the Alps was built in 120 B.C. by the Roman legions themselves across the Pass of the Great St. Bernard. At the summit, the legionnaires built a temple to Jupiter and a hotel for travelers and the crews of repairmen who maintained the road. Another Roman transalpine highway soon followed; it ran from Taurasia (Turin) in Italy, crossed the Alps by the Pass of the Little St. Bernard, and ended at the small village of Vienna. Its strategic importance was demonstrated soon after its construction when Julius Caesar marched his legions along it into Gaul in 58 B.C. By 53 B.C., Caesar and his legions, whose number never exceeded 120,000, had conquered all of Gaul, killing over 1 million of the native inhabitants in the process. He had also, during this time, built an invasion fleet that he used to make two expeditions across the English Channel to Britain. In the course of the second foray, in 54 B.C., a force of 30,000 Romans penetrated Britain as far as the Thames River and defeated a Celtic tribe that had aided Caesar's enemies in Gaul.

The value of the Roman highway system was demonstrated anew in the winter of 52 B.C. when the Gauls, united under a charismatic chieftain named Vercingetorix, rose up against Roman rule. Caesar had returned to Rome, but using various newly constructed Roman roads, he was able to cover more than 100 miles a day up the length of Italy, across the Alps, and into Gaul, where he defeated Vercingetorix at Alesia. The Gauls then adopted a strategy of conducting simultaneous small uprisings at several different locations throughout their country, but the Roman system of four major highways and many more collateral roads, designed by the engineers and architects who followed in the wake of the legions, enabled Caesar to effectively deploy his troops to as many spots as necessary.

Soon all effective resistance to the Romans had been crushed, and all of Gaul was reduced to a peaceful Roman province where substantial towns sprang up alongside the highways throughout the countryside. The major north-south highway from the Mediterranean coast near Massilia ran to the German border at Mainz and Cologne. At Lyons, another highway ran east-west to the Atlantic Ocean through Limoges and Saintes to Bordeaux. In the north, a roadway ran from the English Channel at Boulogne

Roman highways are the most lasting legacy of the great empire; many of them are still in use throughout Europe.

Under the reign of Caesar Augustus and his successors, the ancient world was peacefully united as never before, and travel and commerce flourished. With the fall of the Roman Empire, Europe entered its Dark Ages, and much geographic knowledge was lost; what historians refer to as the First Great Age of Exploration would begin when Renaissance Europe, for reasons of commerce and conquest, again began to look outward beyond its borders and would culminate in the discovery and exploration of the New World.

south-east to Langres, where it connected with the roads to Rome.

Succeeding generations of Romans continued this policy of expansion, conquest, and consolidation, until, by the 3rd century A.D., the Roman Empire encompassed virtually all of the known world of the ancients. Highways spoked out from the city of Rome in 12 different directions and helped enable the Romans to extend their influence to the Balkan Peninsula and the present-day nations of Austria, Hungary, and Romania. Under the so-called Pax Romana (the peace of Rome), which is generally held to have begun during the reign of Caesar Augustus at about the time of the birth of

Christ and to have lasted for 200 years, the ancient world was unified as never before, travelers enjoyed relatively safe passage to even its most remote regions, and the store of geographic knowledge increased many times over. But with Rome's fall in A.D. 453, the ancient world was once again fragmented, and Europe entered its Dark Ages, one manifestation of which was what the historian Daniel Boorstin has called the Great Interruption of Geographical Knowledge. Religious dogma replaced scientific truth and empirical knowledge as the source of geographic information, and much of the knowledge of the ancients—particularly as regarded the mysterious continents of Asia and Africa—was lost, not to be regained until many centuries later, when Marco Polo and his fellow medieval explorers focused attention on lands far beyond the old boundaries of the known world.

Further Reading

Baines, John, and J. Malek. *Atlas of Ancient Egypt*. New York: Facts on File, 1980.

Baker, J. N. L. *A History of Geographical Discovery and Exploration*. New York: Cooper Square, 1967.

Baker, J. Oliver T. *History of Ancient Geography*. New York: Biblio and Tannen, 1965.

Boak, Arthur E., and William Sinnigen. *A History of Rome to* A.D. *565*. New York: Macmillian, 1966.

Bowra, C. M. *Classical Greece*. New York: Time-Life, 1971.

Cary, M., and E. H. Warmington. *The Ancient Explorers*. New York: Dodd, Mead, 1929.

Cornell, Tim, and J. Mathews. *Atlas of the Roman World*. New York: Facts on File, 1982.

Cotrell, Leonard. *Hannibal: Enemy of Rome*. New York: Holt, Rinehart & Winston, 1961.

Dodge, Theodore A. *Great Captains*. Port Washington, NY: Kennicat Press, 1968.

Fox, Robin Lane. *The Search for Alexander*. Boston: Little, Brown, 1980.

Hadas, Moses. *Imperial Rome*. New York: Time-Life, 1965.

Heyerdahl, Thor. *Early Man and the Ocean*. New York: Doubleday, 1979.

Latouche, Robert. *Caesar to Charlemagne*. London: Barnes and Noble, 1968.

Levi, Peter. *Atlas of the Greek World.* New York: Facts on File, 1987.

Mercer, Charles. *Alexander the Great.* New York: American Heritage, 1962.

Newby, Eric. *The World Atlas of Exploration.* New York: Crescent Books, 1975.

Chronology

3200 B.C.	The earliest recorded Egyptian sea voyage is undertaken
1900 B.C.	The Minoan palace of Knossos is built on the island of Crete
1500 B.C.	Egyptians, under the command of Pharaoh Tothmes III, invade Syria
1322 B.C.	Queen Hatshepsut sends a naval expedition to Somalia, the southern tip of the Arabian Peninsula, and, possibly, beyond to the Kuria Muria Islands located off present-day Oman
c. 1200 B.C.	The Greek conquest of Troy begins; Greeks establish colonies on the Black Sea
1110 B.C.	Phoenicians establish a colony at Gades, on the coast of present-day Spain
1101 B.C.	Phoenicians establish a colony at Utica, in present-day Libya
814 B.C.	Dido, the daughter of the King of Tyre, supposedly founds Carthage
c. 800 B.C.	Greek colony of Cumae is established on the west coast of Italy
735 B.C.	Greek colony of Naxos is founded on Sicily
c. 650 B.C.	A Greek merchant named Colaeus happens upon the Phoenician settlement of Tartessus
c. 600 B.C.	Phoenicians circumnavigate the African continent from east to west
546 B.C.	Cyrus the Great, emperor of the Persians, defeats the Lydian king Croesus
401 B.C.	Greek mercenaries known as the Ten Thousand enter the employ of Cyrus; conduct an epic retreat through unfamiliar regions of the Near East
338 B.C.	Philip, king of Macedon, conquers the Greek city-states of Athens and Thebes

325 B.C.	Alexander the Great returns to Greece from India
June 10, 323 B.C.	Alexander the Great dies
c. 310 B.C.	The Greek merchant Pytheas establishes trade with the British Isles
261 B.C.	The first of the three Punic Wars, between Rome and Carthage, begins
241 B.C.	The First Punic War ends
218 B.C.	The Second Punic War begins; the Carthaginian general Hannibal invades the Roman town of Saguntum; Hannibal leads a massive army across Europe, crosses the Alps, and descends upon Italy
201 B.C.	The Second Punic War ends
149 B.C.	The Third Punic War begins
146 B.C.	Carthage falls; the Third Punic War ends
53 B.C.	Caesar conquers Gaul
120 B.C.	The first Roman road through the Alps is constructed
c. 120 B.C.–A.D. 453	Roman roads spoke out from Rome, giving the Roman army the mobility to rule a vast empire
A.D. 453	Fall of Rome

Index

Picture Credits

Ann Gaines has a masters degree in American studies from the University of Texas at Austin and is the author of *Alexander von Humboldt, Colossus of Exploration* and *John Wesley Powell and the Great Surveys of the American West* in this series.

William H. Goetzmann holds the Jack S. Blanton, Sr., Chair in History at the University of Texas at Austin, where he has taught for many years. The author of numerous works on American history and exploration, he won the 1967 Pulitzer and Parkman prizes for his *Exploration and Empire: The Role of the Explorer and Scientist in the Winning of the American West, 1800–1900*. With his son William N. Goetzmann, he coauthored *The West of the Imagination*, which received the Carr P. Collins Award in 1986 from the Texas Institute of Letters. His documentary television series of the same name received a blue ribbon in the history category at the American Film and Video Festival held in New York City in 1987. A recent work, *New Lands, New Men: America and the Second Great Age of Discovery*, was published in 1986 to much critical acclaim.

Michael Collins served as command module pilot on the *Apollo 11* space mission, which landed his colleagues Neil Armstrong and Buzz Aldrin on the moon. A graduate of the United States Military Academy, Collins was named an astronaut in 1963. In 1966 he piloted the *Gemini 10* mission, during which he became the third American to walk in space. The author of several books on space exploration, Collins was director of the Smithsonian Institution's National Air and Space Museum from 1971 to 1978 and is a recipient of the Presidential Medal of Freedom.